WEBSITE
DESIGN
MADE EASY

Publisher and Creative Director: Nick Wells
Commissioning Editor: Polly Prior
Project Editor: Josie Mitchell
Art Director and Layout Design: Mike Spender
Digital Design and Production: Chris Herbert
Copy Editor: Anna Groves
Screenshots: Richard N. Williams
Proofreader: Amanda Leigh
Indexer: Helen Snaith

FLAME TREE PUBLISHING
6 Melbray Mews
London SW6 3NS
United Kingdom

www.flametreepublishing.com
First published 2018

18 20 22 21 19
1 3 5 7 9 10 8 6 4 2

Every effort has been made to contact copyright holders. In the event of an oversight
the publishers would be glad to rectify any omissions in future editions of this book.

A CIP record for this book is available from the British Library upon request.

ISBN 978-1-78664-791-7

Printed in China | Created, Developed & Produced in the United Kingdom

All non-screenshot pictures are courtesy of Shutterstock and © the following photographers: Rawpixel.com: 1, 4, 6, 9, 10, 14, 51, 60, 72,
78, 86, 113, 158, 166, 189, 196, 253; NicoElNino: 3, 49; mirtmirt: 5, 58, 81; wavebreakmedia: 5, 94, 121; NPFire: 6, 128; Africa Studio:
7, 171, 202; Roman Samborskyi: 7, 236; Mr. Kosal: 8; linlypu: 11; RAYBON: 13; Viewvie: 16; Pressmaster: 18; gdainti: 27; garagestock: 31;
Sachezi: 33; funkyfrogstock: 73; SFIO CRACHO: 74; Bokeh Art Photo: 80; n_fransua: 83; tovovan: 84; Botond1977: 85; Olivier Le Moal:
89; garagestock: 92; zdanil: 92; REDPIXEL.PL: 99; one photo: 117; Likoper: 170; baranq: 172; karen roach: 177; iJeab: 184; baranq: 186;
Georgejmclittle: 195; perfectlab: 207; veron_ice: 212; Eloku: 226; ESB Professional: 242; Jiffy Avril: 251.

WEBSITE
DESIGN
MADE EASY

RICHARD N. WILLIAMS

**FLAME TREE
PUBLISHING**

CONTENTS

What is web design, what does it entail? For that matter, what is the Web, how do web browsers work and how do you construct a website to meet the demands of the modern web user?

Learn the basic principles of designing a website, what a homepage is, how a website is structured and the importance of readability and usability.

You can create a simple website without learning code or using complicated software platforms thanks to many online web design platforms and website templates.

INTERMEDIATE WEBSITE DESIGN

For those wanting to create a more sophisticated website, learn how to use many of the software platforms used by professional web designers to create your own website from scratch.

ADVANCED WEBSITE DESIGN

In this chapter you will learn how to create a website using HTML, JavaScript and Cascading Style Sheets (CSS). This is the purest form of web design.

ADDING TO YOUR WEBSITE ..

Learn how to add multimedia, tables and dynamic content to provide your web visitors with the best experience possible, as well as how to create business and e-commerce websites.

TECHNICAL MATTERS ..

From maintenance and troubleshooting to learning about your legal responsibilities, there is more to web design than just creating a website and going live.

INTRODUCTION

Whether you are running a business at home, are involved in a club or charity, require a personal web page, or need an online presence for a business, designing your own website can be fun, exciting and rewarding.

WEB DESIGN

Designing websites is fun and exciting, but it can also be very technical, especially for somebody new to web design. However, these days web design is not just for those familiar with coding, the internet and computers in general.

Various online tools, software programs and other resources mean that nearly anybody can design a website, even if you do not know the difference between HTML, JavaScript and CSS (we'll explain all about these web languages later in this book). The only real difficulty comes in knowing how to effectively present your ideas.

GOOD WEB DESIGN

Good web design is hard to define. Whether a website is well or badly designed can be subjective, but there are agreed ideas of what you should and should not do. Guidelines and standards have been developed to assist web designers in creating more user-friendly pages. It is imperative to understand the motivation behind such rules rather than blindly applying them.

It is a common misconception that style is all that matters in web design. What happens behind the scenes is just as important as how the website looks up front, and it is essential to understand the theory behind why a site works. When it comes to web design, the first rule is to always think of your users, identify who they are, what they want and how you can best serve them.

Usability

Usability plays a crucial part in the effectiveness of a website and is directly related to user satisfaction. Meeting user needs and expectations is the key focus of user-oriented design, although it can be difficult to achieve that fine balance between designer wants and user needs.

Design

Creativity is important, but you do not need to be an expert in graphic design or hold a diploma in art to be a good web designer. Some of the best websites are simple, neat, clean and easy to use, but that doesn't mean they are easy to create. Web design requires careful planning, and the key to creating a successful website lies in having a sound knowledge of all the factors influencing web design and in understanding how to achieve an effective balance between them.

USING THIS BOOK

This book covers all aspects of web design and aims to give readers a wider practical and theoretical knowledge of the field. In this book you will find all the information you will need, whether you are new to web design and want to create personal web pages, such as a family site sharing news and photos, or you are more experienced and want to update a company or e-commerce website.

Jargon Buster

Web design has its own terminology. Where possible we will try to ensure this book is easy to follow, but where complex terms are used, we've included these handy jargon busters.

This book, however, is not designed to teach you how to code – although we will show you lots of different web languages and how best to implement them. If you want to learn to code, we will show you the basics and point you to some resources where you can learn in more detail how to code using the various web languages.

From Beginners to Experts

We will try to cover all you need to design and create your own website, from basic terminology and the various ways in which websites are designed, to the fundamental principles of good web design, as well as attempting to provide you with the inspiration for you to design your own site.

Hot Tip

Throughout this book, we have inserted a number of hot tips. These are designed to give you some simple yet effective advice on different aspects of web design.

This book will also outline some of the best tools for web design, from simple online web creators for creating basic websites, to various software packages that will let you design websites, manipulate images and create dynamic content.

Web Design Made Easy

You can read this book from cover to cover, or you can use it as a reference and turn to it whenever you need help with a particular aspect of web design. This book is designed to help you both build a basic website from scratch and improve the design and structure of existing websites.

This book is full of examples and step-by-step guides to help make even the more complicated aspects of web design easy to accomplish. You will find plenty of labelled diagrams, advice, tips and tricks to help you create, structure and design a website, as well as more advanced information on monetizing a website, optimizing for search engines and how to launch and test your web pages.

THE BASICS OF WEB DESIGN

WHAT IS A WEBSITE?

We all use them, whether shopping online or chatting to friends on social media, but what exactly is a website and what are the different components that allow us to surf the Web?

THE INTERNET AND WORLD WIDE WEB

A lot of people think the terms internet and World Wide Web are interchangeable. They are not. The internet is the name given to the massive network of computers that are all connected together allowing all of us to communicate from our computers, phones or tablets. The World Wide Web (abbreviated to WWW or the Web) are the pages on the internet that we all use.

Below: The World Wide Web is made up of millions upon millions of different web pages.

While the internet has been around for decades, it wasn't until English scientist Tim Berners-Lee invented the World Wide Web in 1989 that it started to become the internet as we now know it.

COMPONENTS OF THE WEB

The Web consists of millions and millions of websites and web pages, all of which are interconnected with links. These links form the pathways that allow search engines and other websites to connect with a web page. Without this web of links, the internet would be unable to find a website without knowing its exact web address.

Jargon Buster

A website address is often called a URL (Uniform Resource Locator). URLs contain the location of a website and the protocol needed to access it, such as HTTP.

Hot Tip

All website addresses begin with the prefix http:// or https:// – Hyper Text Transfer Protocol (Secure) – and are often followed by www (World Wide Web).

https://www.google.co.uk/search?rlz=1C2(

ome Thesaurus a KDP Sales

Above: Hyper Text Transfer Protocol (HTTP) precedes every web address.

HTTP

Hypertext Transfer Protocol (HTTP) is the standard set of rules, or protocol, for passing files and other information (collectively known as resources) around the Web. These resources could be text, image files, query results or anything else. HTTP transfers the content of a web page to a browser's computer by sending it in packets. Once all these packets are received, a web page is visible on a user's computer. This means when we 'visit' a website we are not visiting it at all but in effect downloading an exact copy to our computer.

Because of this, websites have to work on various types of computers and devices, some of which may be running different software. These can range from PCs and Apple Mac desktop computers, to mobile phones, tablets and laptops.

Browsers

Access to the World Wide Web is through a web browser. Browsers are just software packages that can navigate the Web and translate the HTML code (more on this a little later) that creates web pages into the text and images you see on screen. There are a number of browsers for PCs, Macs, phones and tablets, so web pages not only have to work on different devices but also on different browsers.

These are the most commonly used browsers:

- **Internet Explorer**: Microsoft's Internet Explorer is often found running on a Windows PC, but it is available for other devices.

- **Safari**: This is Apple's web browser for both its Mac computers and iOS smartphones and tablets.

- **Chrome**: Google's web browser is available for PC and Mac as well as iOS and Android smartphones and tablets.

Below: Google's Chrome is now the most popular browser.

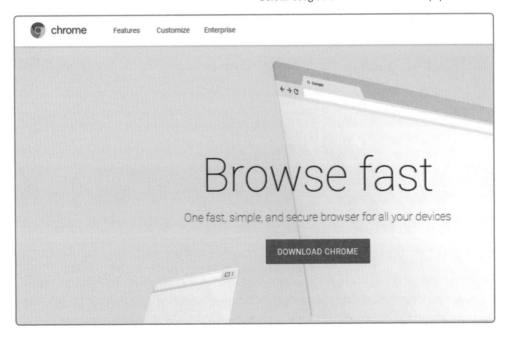

Domains

All web pages have a domain name. This is often based on the company or website it belongs to and is the main part of the URL. For instance, microsoft.com is the domain name that identifies the web pages for software company Microsoft. The .com suffix is known as a 'top-level domain' and reflects the type of organization and country the site belongs to, such as .com for commercial organizations, .co.uk for UK websites, and .org for non-profit bodies.

IP Addresses

Domain names are really a convenience for web users. To locate a site on the internet, the domain name needs to be translated into its IP address. This is a block of four numbers separated by periods, and is translated by DNS servers (Domain Name System), which find the IP address for each domain, locating the website for you.

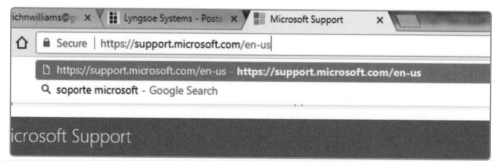

Above: A URL contains the protocol, domain name, any sub domains, and a top-level domain such as .com.

WEB HOSTING

The communication with a website is a client-host relationship. The client is an internet user's computer wanting to download a web page while the website is on a host server. To be live on the Web, a website needs to be hosted; this simply means finding a server to put it on.

Web Servers

Web servers are not hard to find. A large number of companies will offer to host your website for you. Some of these are free, others cost; some offer additional features you may or may not need.

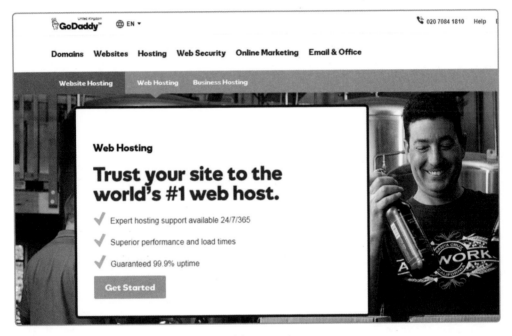

Above: Companies such as GoDaddy offer various web-hosting packages.

Types of Hosting

Shared hosting: Often this is free or very low-cost but you will have to share the server with other websites and have your host's domain name as part of your URL.

Dedicated server: With a dedicated server, you do not have to worry about other websites taking up resources and you can use your own domain name, but you have to pay more.

➔ **Virtual Private Servers (VPS):** These share a physical server but unlike shared hosting you can often use your own domain name and are allocated a set amount of resources.

Which Web Server?

The web server that suits your website will depend on a number of factors.

➔ **Traffic:** If you are expecting large numbers of visitors to your website, you may want to consider a dedicated server.

➔ **Domain name:** If you do not mind your website being a sub-domain of the hosting company and you do not expect lots of visitors, shared hosting could be the best option.

➔ **Files:** If you want to host large files or run a lot of programs on your website, a shared service may be too limited.

Above: The cost of web hosting often depends on the amount of storage and bandwidth you need.

HTML: BACKBONE OF THE WEB

HTML is everywhere on the World Wide Web. It makes up every website and web page, but what is it and how much do you need to know?

HYPERTEXT MARK-UP LANGUAGE

HTML is the language of the Web. It is used to construct web pages. In effect, it tells the browser software how to display and handle the information or objects contained on a web page. It also controls the hypertext links that enable you to click from one document to another or from one section of a page to another.

HTML Documents

A website is essentially an HTML document containing all the information about how it should appear and operate. Each HTML document has two main parts: the Head, which contains general information about the file and scripts that need to be run; and the Body, where the content will appear in the browser window.

Below: All websites are created using HTML code.

```
1  <!DOCTYPE html>
2  <html lang="en-GB">
3
4  <head>
5    <meta name="viewport" content="width=device-width, initial-scale=1">
6
7    <title>- GoDaddy UK</title>
8  <meta charset="utf-8">
9  <meta name="description" content="">
10 <meta name="google-site-verification" content="t7JT1iH2iscenNr74R-kgXP1jL_ru6OPiT9RE8zDk04">
11 <meta name="msvalidate.01" content="2E3FEEF3C657AC432E75D756D93E3175">
12 <meta name="robots" content="NOINDEX, NOFOLLOW">
13
14 <link rel="canonical" href="https://uk.godaddy.com/offers/web-hosting">
15 <link rel="shortcut icon" href="https://img1.wsimg.com/Sitecore/3/A/4/{3A44F70D-6D11-4C14-B611-A1F1917
16 <meta property="og:title" content="- GoDaddy UK">
17 <meta property="og:description" content="">
18 <meta property="og:type" content="product">
19 <meta property="og:url" content="https://uk.godaddy.com/offers/web-hosting">
20 <meta property="og:image" content="https://img1.wsimg.com/Sitecore/D/7/og-social-dlp-offer-hosting-mvp
21 <meta property="og:site_name" content="GoDaddy">
```

HTML CODE

Many software packages and resources are available to help you create a website without you needing to know any HTML, but HTML is not a complex code. As such, you do not need to be a computer expert to learn basic HTML, and knowing some HTML can help when it comes to designing or making changes to your website.

Hot Tip

To make website text bold you use the `<b>bold</b>` tags. To make something italic you use the `<i>italic</i>` tag.

HTML Tags

All HTML documents are collections of tags, enclosed within less than (<) and greater than (>) brackets and usually closed with a backslash (/). Tags allow you to specify properties such as font, size and colour for text contained between the tags. Tags are also used to display files such as images.

```
    <div class="plan-image  text-left"
        data-same-size='{"group":"mod-grp-7a17a99f-6212-4
image","match":"height","disableHeightBelow":"0"}'>

    </div>
    <div class="plan-title headline-primary h2 plan-tile-t
        data-same-size='{"group":"mod-grp-7a17a99f-6212-4
title","match":"height","disableHeightBelow":"0"}'>
        Economy
    </div>
    <div class="plan-text  text-left"
        data-same-size='{"group":"mod-grp-7a17a99f-6212-4
text","match":"height","disableHeightBelow":"0"}'>

    </div>
```

Above: The < and > symbols are used a lot in HTML.

Essential Tags

Every HTML file, and so every website, requires four sets of HTML tags that are needed to form the basic structure:

```
<head>
  <meta name="viewport" content="wid

  <title>- GoDaddy UK</title>
<meta charset="utf-8">
<meta name="description" content="">
<meta name="google-site-verification
<meta name="msvalidate.01" content="
```

Above: The title tag contains the name of the web page as it appears in a web browser.

- **HTML:** The `<html></html>` tags identify the beginning and end of the HTML document. All other tags must fall between the html tags.

- **Head:** The `<head></head>` tags contain information about the document that will not appear on the actual page, such as the title of the document, the author and which style sheet to use (more on style sheets later).

- **Title:** The `<title></title>` tags contain the title that will appear in the title bar of a web browser when somebody visits your website.

- **Body:** The `<body></body>` tags contain all the information that is visible on the page. All your text, images and links must go between these tags.

Headers

HTML lets you set up websites under a header. HTML has six headers, denoted by the tags <h1> to <h6> with <h1> being the most important. Headings let you apply font changes, paragraph breaks before and after, and any white space necessary to render the heading. Headers are used by search engines to index the contents of your website, as well as by readers who use them to navigate a web page to find the information they are looking for.

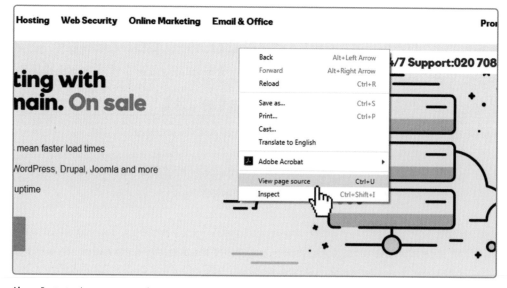

Above: By viewing the page source in a browser you can see the HTML document containing all the information that has created the web page.

OTHER WEB LANGUAGES

HTML alone cannot provide everything a browser needs to create a website. Often web pages have files in them, such as images or documents. For this reason, a website may need several other languages to help create it.

Cascading Style Sheets

CSS, short for Cascading Style Sheets, is a language that describes how HTML elements are to be displayed on screen. Using CSS can save a lot of work as it can control the layout of multiple web pages all at once.

JavaScript

Commonly used for websites that require user interaction, JavaScript is a programming language that allows scripts from users' computers (clients) to interact on a website. If you require any input from a user on your website, such as typing in information, you will need to use JavaScript.

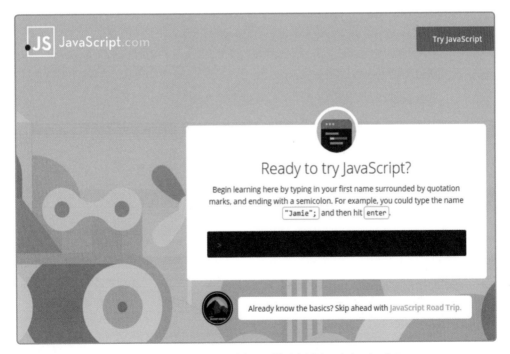

Above: There are other programming languages behind the World Wide Web, including JavaScript.

HTML5

HTML is continually developed and the latest version was released in November 2014. HTML5.1 has more support for video. Previously, the only way to run videos on a website was to use plug-in technologies, such as Adobe Flash, which allows web developers to incorporate animations and interactive elements.

Web Files

Websites do not just contain text; all sorts of files are used to create websites and provide information. These include:

Jargon Buster

Plug-ins are software systems that add extra features to another program, such as a web browser.

⊖ **Image files:** The most widely used formats on websites are GIF, JPG and PNG.

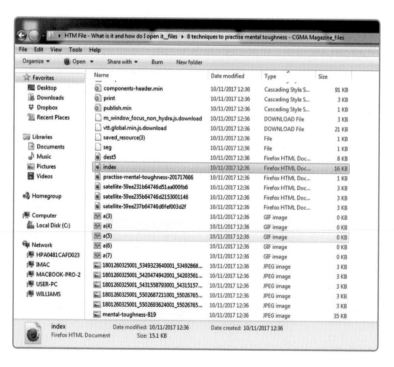

⊖ **Multimedia:** Video and music files such as MP3 and MP4 can be played on a website using a plug-in or by embedding them.

⊖ **PDF:** You can also upload PDF files to your website and allow users to view them.

Left: When you save a web page, you can see all the different files that make it up.

A WEBSITE AS A FILE

A website written in HTML is not a very big file. All the HTML that is used to create a website can be viewed on programs such as Microsoft Notepad. However, many of the features of a website, such as images, videos, multimedia and banners, need to be stored alongside the HTML information.

HTML Files

A basic web page is stored as a text file, although it is given the file extension of .html (or sometimes .htm depending on your operating system). However, when you save a website, all the files used to create it, including the .html files, images and other multimedia, need to be saved as a collection of files and folders.

Jargon Buster

A file extension is just the digits after the dot in a filename that describes the type of file it is. A .txt file is a text file, an .htm file is an HTML document, a .jpg file is an image and so on.

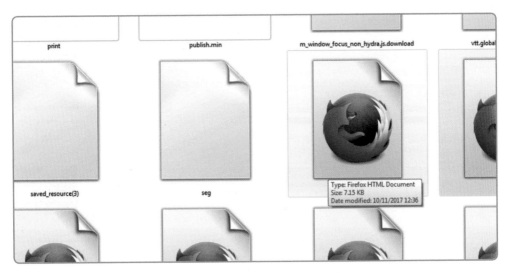

print

publish.min

m_window_focus_non_hydra.js.download

vtt.global

saved_resource(3)

seg

Type: Firefox HTML Document
Size: 7.15 KB
Date modified: 10/11/2017 12:36

Above: Your browser will recognize an .htm file as an HTML document.

WHAT IS WEB DESIGN?

What does web design entail? What skills do you need? How much does designing a website cost? These can be difficult questions to answer as web design can vary in complexity and cost.

BUILDING A WEBSITE

Websites used to be very difficult to create, requiring coding skills and often the help of a professional website designer. Things have changed. You no longer need any coding knowledge to create a website. There are lots of resources to do all the hard work for you. All you need is a little creativity and a good idea of what you want to achieve.

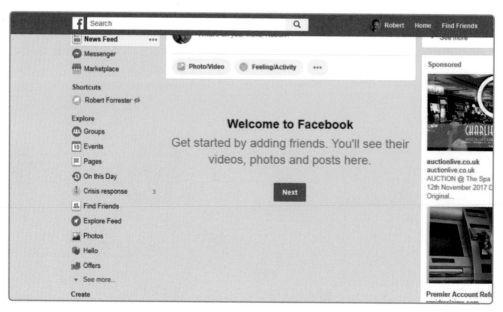

Above: Every website, even Facebook as shown here, has been designed by somebody.

ASPECTS OF WEB DESIGN

Web design covers all aspects of creating websites, including the web page layout, content production and graphic design. Some web designers create websites from scratch, typing out HTML and other codes, other web designers use software systems to build their own website from the ground up. There are also online platforms and templates that can give you a good starting point.

Hot Tip

If you are going to design your own website, you need to be prepared. Before you begin, collect all the information, images and other resources you want your website to contain.

Skills

The skills required to design a website vary from simple computer skills if you use a website template, to a range of skill levels that include:

- **Design**: As its name suggests, a lot of web design requires design skills, knowing where items should be placed on a page, what looks good, how well something functions, and knowing what fonts, colours and icons to use.

- **Web knowledge**: Knowing how the Web works can be a major advantage for web designers, including a grasp of SEO (search engine optimization), what plug-ins do, how browsers display HTML and so on.

Above: Web design can be improved with knowledge of things such as search engine optimization.

Software: Web design can require the use of multiple software systems, from content management systems (CMS), such as WordPress, to design software, such as Dreamweaver and Photoshop.

Content creation: Being able to write content, source images and translate information is important when building a website.

GET CREATIVE

Whether you can code a website from scratch, manipulate pictures in image-editing software or can only move content around on a website template, the great thing about web design is that it is available to all skill levels.

Above: When creating a website you may find yourself using programs such as Photoshop or Paint.NET.

MAKE A PLAN

Before you start looking for web-development tools, domain names, web-hosting companies and other things, it is a good idea to have an approximate idea of what type of website you want to design:

- ➔ **Purpose**: Identify the purpose of your website. Decide who it is aimed at and what subject matter it will contain. Search the Web for sites covering the same topics or business rivals, and decide how your site will be different.

- ➔ **Structure**: Create a basic section structure. What will be on each page? How many pages will you need to create?

- ➔ **Colour and type**: Think about colours and typefaces. If you are creating a business website, do you have brand colours? Think about styles and whether you want a professional or friendly tone.

Right: Create a plan. You should know how many pages you want and what you want on each page.

HOW TO BUILD A WEBSITE

How you choose to build your website will depend on a number of factors, such as budget, how much knowledge of HTML you have, and how you want your website to look and function. You can design and build a website in one of three ways:

⊖   **Basic**: Online web tools, usually provided by web-hosting companies, let you design a website online and require no coding knowledge.

⊖   **Intermediate**: Web-development software downloaded from the internet will let you design a website, maybe from an existing template, requiring some but not many coding skills.

⊖   **Expert**: You can build a website simply by writing out the code in a program such as Microsoft Notepad.

```
Notes - Notepad
File  Edit  Format  View  Help
})();
</script>
<noscript>
<p><img alt="Clicky" width="1" height="1" src="//in.getclicky.com/207602ns.gif" /></p>
</noscript>
<script type="text/javascript" src="//apis.google.com/js/plusone.js">
   {lang: 'en-GB'}
</script>

<script type="text/javascript">
   var _gaq = _gaq || [];
   _gaq.push(['_setAccount', 'UA-31791909-1']);
   _gaq.push(['_trackPageview']);

   (function() {
      var ga = document.createElement('script'); ga.type = 'text/javascript'; ga.async = true;
      ga.src = ('https:' == document.location.protocol ? 'https://ssl' : 'http://www') + '.google-analyti
      var s = document.getElementsByTagName('script')[0]; s.parentNode.insertBefore(ga, s);
   })();
</script>
<script type="text/javascript">
if (document.referrer.match(/google\.com/gi) && document.referrer.match(/cd/gi)) {
   var myString = document.referrer;
   var r        = myString.match(/cd=(.*?)&/);
   var rank     = parseInt(r[1]);
   var kw       = myString.match(/q=(.*?)&/);

   if (kw[1].length > 0) {
      var keyWord  = decodeURI(kw[1]);
   } else {
      keyWord = "(not provided)";
   }

   var p        = document.location.pathname;
```

Above: You can use programs such as Microsoft Notepad to write code out manually.

COSTS

Your budget for creating and designing a website can often affect the choices you make about where you host your website and how you create it. The costs for creating and running a website include:

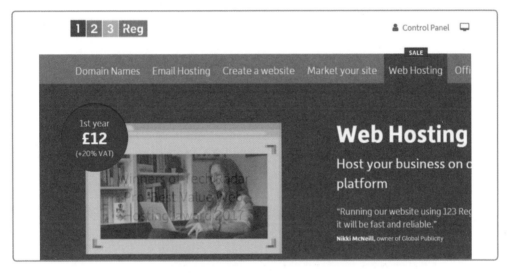

Above: Having a website may involve fixed costs such as web hosting.

→ **Domain name registration**: If you want your own domain name, this will need to be bought and registered.

→ **Hosting**: Web-hosting costs vary hugely depending on many factors, and will be an ongoing monthly or yearly cost.

→ **Web design**: Perhaps the highest cost for a web owner is having the website built. Creating it yourself may mean you have to buy your own software or use a free web-creation platform.

→ **Content**: Images, videos and so on may be under copyright, so you may have to buy licenses to use them.

WEB DESIGN MADE EASY

Even if you have never learned HTML or other web languages, it is still possible to create your own website thanks to many online and downloadable services and programs.

GOING BASIC

Designing a website can be very simple thanks to many web-building tools. These do the hard work for you by handling all HTML and other languages. You simply tell the tool how you want each web page to look and it converts your requests into web code. It can take less than an hour to have a fully functional website, meaning you can have your website online sooner.

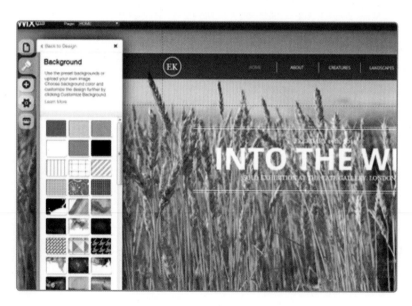

Above: WYSIWYG editors create the code for you so you can design a website just like designing any other document.

WYSIWYG

Many web design tools use the principal of WYSIWYG ('what you see is what you get'). As WYSIWYG web editors, they let you build and view the web pages you create graphically, just as they will appear in the browser. You can draw tables, add images and set up text styles without ever looking at the HTML code or typing in a tag.

ONLINE WEBSITE DESIGN TOOLS

There are many online platforms that will let you create a website. Many of these are free and most are provided by web-hosting companies. It means you can create a website and have it uploaded to the internet straightaway with the web-hosting company handling the domain name, URL and everything else that is required.

Popular Online Web Tools

- **Wix**: www.wix.com. Provides a website builder for hosting on their site. They also have hundreds of website templates but you have to use them on their site.

> **Hot Tip**
>
> If you are thinking of using a web design tool provided by a web-hosting company, shop around as hosting fees can vary.

- **WordPress**: www.wordpress. com. Originally a blogging platform, now used by many web developers to design and create websites.

- **Weebly**: www. weebly.com. A web-hosting company whose web builder uses a simple drag-and-drop system.

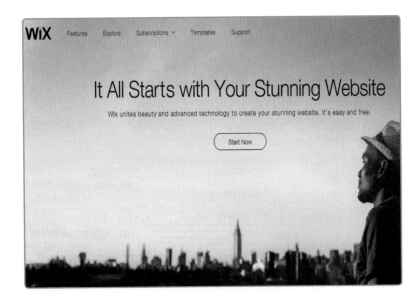

Above: Wix.com provides templates and a WYSIWYG web tool that lets you build a website.

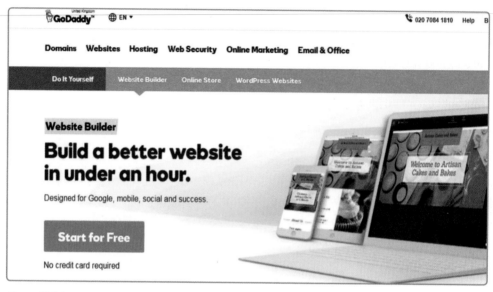

Above: Web-hosting companies such as GoDaddy have their own website building tools.

GoDaddy: www.uk.godaddy.com. One of the most popular web-hosting companies in the UK, it also has a simple-to-use web builder.

Squarespace: www.squarespace.com. A content management software service that provides an integrated website builder, blogging platform, hosting service, commerce platform and domain name registrar.

THINGS TO CONSIDER

There are so many web-hosting companies offering so many different services that establishing what value they offer for your money requires some consideration. Ensure they provide all the hosting services you need, and check they can provide the bandwidth, domain and storage options you need. You may also find you have to accept the web-hosting company's domain name, which may not be something you want to do.

Constraints

Simplicity does come at a cost. Most online website development tools are limited in scope. You may find your creativity constrained or you may want to make minor changes but the constraints of the web design tool mean you cannot. You may also want a website to perform a task not built into the web design tool.

WEBSITE TEMPLATES

Another easy method of designing a website is to use a template. Templates are fully functional websites to which you just add text and replace the basic information to make it your own. You can download website templates easily on the Web, and some are offered free. The only downside to templates is the risk of your website looking very similar to other people's. If you are after originality, using these templates may not be for you.

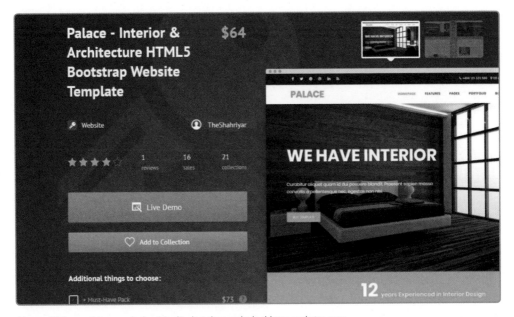

Above: Web templates may lack originality but they make building a website easy.

Using Templates

Templates do offer some freedom. You do not have to structure a web template the way you receive it. You can adjust the colours, fonts, images, graphics and content, as well as move elements around. This may require additional skills, although online resources make editing a template quite simple.

Hot Tip

Choose a web-hosting company and see if they have a website builder. If they do not, shop around to find somebody that does who is charging similar hosting fees.

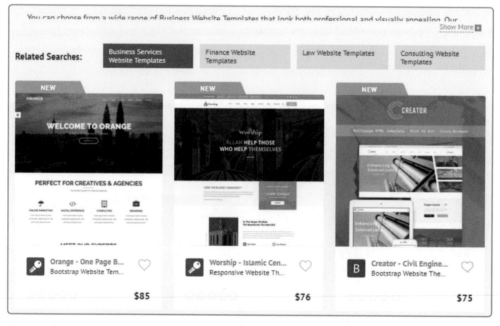

Above: You can often find web templates ordered by business type, providing the basic style and structure for a specific industry.

Website Template Resources

You can find templates very easily on the Web. Some are free, some are costly and they vary from simplistic to sophisticated, allowing for a number of features.

- **Squarespace**: Free templates can also be downloaded from www.squarespace.com/templates.

- **TemplateMonster**: You can find hundreds of website templates at varying prices at www.templatemonster.com.

- **Creative Market**: Offers nearly 3,000 website templates for portfolio, blog or corporate websites. Find it at https://creativemarket.com/templates/websites.

COSTS

Using a template or an online website creation tool can be the most inexpensive way to get a website up and running. While some website templates can cost, there are plenty of free resources out there and no shortage of free online web creation tools.

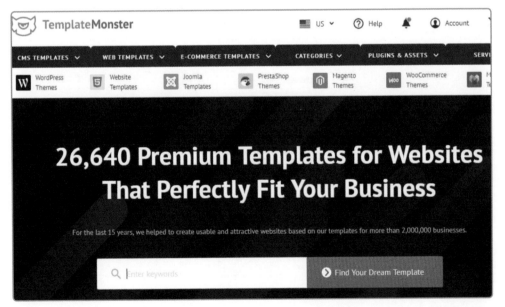

Above: TemplateMonster hosts a large number of templates for businesses or personal websites, so you're sure to find one you like.

SOFTWARE TOOLS

You may want to create a more sophisticated website than the templates and web creation tools allow. This is entirely possible, you just need the right software.

WEB DESIGN SOFTWARE

For those who want more features than those offered by online web creation platforms, but do not want to create a website by typing code into a text document, a professional web design platform could be the answer. These enable you to create any type of website with whatever features you want, but these programs do have a learning curve, and to get the best out of them a little knowledge of HTML, CSS and other coding may help.

WYSIWYG

These software programs still operate under the principal of WYSIWYG. In other words you can see what your website will look like as you create it. However, they also allow you to delve into the code and allow far more features. In fact, the possibilities are endless and programs such as Adobe Dreamweaver have become the Web equivalent of page layout tools like InDesign, often used in publishing.

Left: Adobe Dreamweaver is a popular web design software tool.

BUYING SOFTWARE

Having your own software brings with it many advantages. Web design software is often more sophisticated than the online creation platforms and gives you far more freedom than you get using a template. While some software is free to download and use, the more sophisticated programs can be expensive.

Web Design Software

You can use all sorts of different software for all sorts of different purposes when designing websites, but a number of web design programs provide many of the functions you need to structure, design, lay out and save your website to working files. These vary in complexity, functionality and price. Most provide a WYSIWYG code editor and a live view so you can see how your website changes when modifications are made.

Below: Web design software lets you see and edit the HTML code as well as giving you a WYSIWYG view.

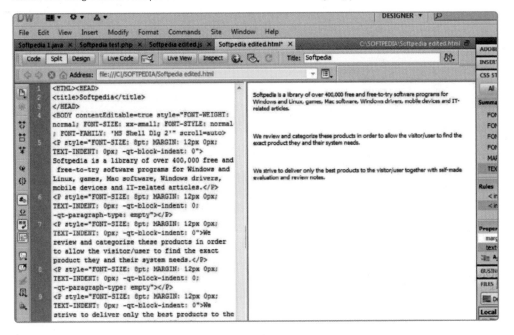

POPULAR PROGRAMS

There are a number of web design development tools.
Here are some of the most popular:

 **Adobe Dreamweaver CC**: £19.97/$19.99 per
month; www.adobe.com/uk/products/dreamweaver.
Dreamweaver in various guises has long been the
program of choice for professional web developers.

 **BlueGriffon**: Free; https://bluegriffon.en.softonic.
com. A free web editor that offers many of the same
features as Dreamweaver but can be simpler to use.

Jargon Buster

Content Management Systems (CMS – not to be confused with CSS), are software platforms used to manage digital content, such as the components and pages of a website.

Above: The free program BlueGriffon offers many of the same features as professional software such as Dreamweaver.

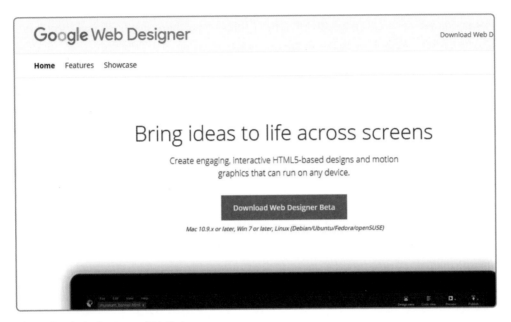

Above: Google also has its own Web Designer.

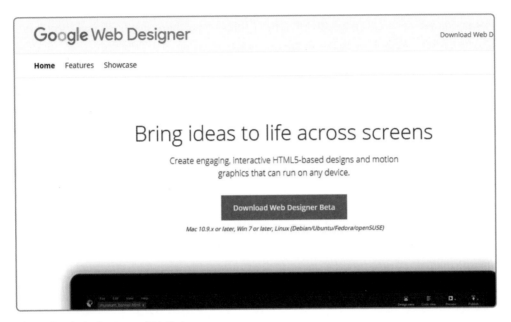 **Google Web Designer:** Free; www.google.co.uk/webdesigner/. A free tool provided by Google to help you create HTML5 web content that fits any device.

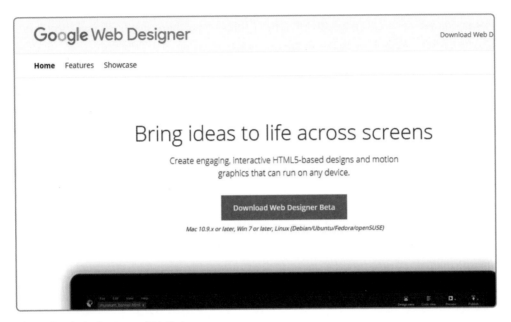 **WordPress:** Free; www.wordpress.com. While strictly speaking a content management platform, WordPress does have a WYSIWYG web design system.

Using a Web Design Program

Software such as Dreamweaver or BlueGriffon lets you build a complete website from scratch, and have it exported to actual working website files. You do not need any understanding of code, but the more you have, the more complicated you can

Hot Tip

One note of caution: while your page may look good in the preview browser of your WYSIWYG HTML editor, that is no guarantee it is going to look the same for visitors accessing your site through a variety of browsers on different devices.

make your web design. Usually with this type of software you have split or separate windows, one for code and one showing the actual graphical page view.

These tools allow you to create your website and see the actual code being added. Alternatively you can choose to insert code and see the changes in real life. You can add content by uploading it from your computer, dragging and dropping in place, or by entering the code.

Disadvantages

Using software such as BlueGriffon or Dreamweaver gives you so much more freedom than an online web creation tool or template. There is no limit to the sorts of websites you can create, but all this creativity does come at a cost in terms of both time and money. Even if you are using a free program, it can take many hours to create a website from the ground up. Of course, you can use the software to make changes to an existing template, which may be quicker.

```html
<!DOCTYPE html>
<html class="google mmfb" lang="en-GB">
  <head>
    <meta charset="utf-8">
    <script>
    (function(H){H.className=H.className.replace(/\bgoogle\b/,'google-js')})(document.documentElement)
    </script>
    <meta content="initial-scale=1, minimum-scale=1, width=device-width" name="viewport">
    <meta content=
    "Google Web Designer is a free, professional-grade HTML5 authoring tool. Build interactive, animated HTML5 creative, r
    name="description">
    <title>
      Google Web Designer
    </title>
    <script src="//www.google.com/js/google.js"></script>
    <link href=
    "//fonts.googleapis.com/css?family=Open+Sans:300,400,600,700|Product+Sans:400&amp;lang=en" rel=
    "stylesheet">
    <link href="/webdesigner/css/default.min.css" rel="stylesheet">
    <link href="//www.google.com/webdesigner/images/favicon.ico" rel="shortcut icon" type=
    "image/x-icon">
  </head>
  <body>
    <div class="maia-header" id="maia-header" role="banner">
      <div class="maia-aux">
```

Above: Web design programs may not produce code as cleanly as a coding it yourself.

For an experienced coder, programs that convert content into HTML can often leave bits of unnecessary code, or use different code than a human coder would. This can make the website 'less clean', which can raise issues with SEO (*see* pages 92–93) and page loading speed.

OTHER SOFTWARE

While web design software can be used to design the look and feel of a website, other aspects of web design may require you to use other software systems.

↪ **Image software**: You may have to create your own graphics and images. Software such as Adobe Photoshop can help you manipulate, edit and create images.

↪ **Content Management Systems (CMS)**: A website with lots of content may need to be managed by a content management system. Some web-hosting services provide CMS systems, but many web developers choose to use something such as WordPress or Joomla.

Above: The CMS platform, WordPress, is also one of the most popular tools for building and managing websites.

➔ **Other programs:** You may wish to use the spell checker on word-processing software such as Microsoft Word when writing web content, or use graphic design software such as Adobe Illustrator to create image content.

Things to Remember

If you are buying software, it is worth bearing in mind that it could be under licence. That is, you may have to pay an annual fee to use the software. If you are buying lots of different software packages to build just one website, the costs can soon add up, but there are plenty of free options out there. In addition, software platforms all have a learning curve and you may have to spend some time learning to use them, so make sure you take advantage of any free trial period to ensure you are making the right purchase.

Below: You can save things you create on programs such as Microsoft Word in a web page format to make publishing to the web easier.

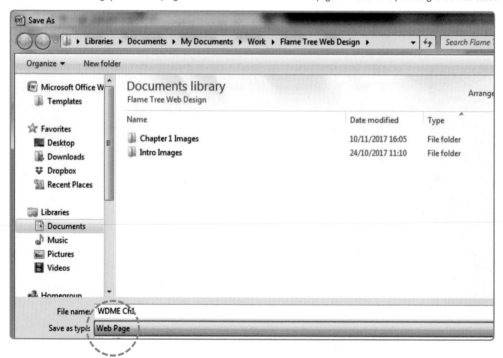

HTML CODING AND EDITING

For purists and those wanting to take their web development to the next level, hand coding can maximize the control you have over the look of your web pages.

CODING

All programs and files are created on computers using code, and websites are no different. Simply put, code is a language used to relay instructions to a computer or program to complete certain tasks. In fact, language and code are often synonymous in computer coding.

Codes

The world of computer coding is full of codes. Operating systems, programs, files, documents and so on all require code. Different languages are developed to get computers to do different tasks.

For websites the main languages are:

- ➔ **HTML**: Used to create the basic structure and content of a web page.

- ➔ **JavaScript**: Used to create interactive elements on a web page.

- ➔ **CSS**: Used for the design of a web page, providing better placement and design capabilities than HTML.

Hot Tip

Web designers also use other codes such as PHP, SQL, Ruby, Python, and C++. There's a lot of crossover in what these languages can do, but each will have its own unique properties.

```
<!ctype html><html itemscope="" itemtype="http://schema.org/WebPage" lang="en-GB"><head><meta content="/images/branding/googleg/1x/googleg_
nprop="image"><link href="/images/branding/product/ico/googleg_lodp.ico" rel="shortcut icon"><meta content="origin" id="mref" name="refer
nction(){window.google=
1:'S88FWsSKMYeaU87bksAK',kEXPI:'201793,1354277,1354443,1354723,1354915,1355220,1355675,1355736,1355866,1356031,1356079,1356370,3300011,334
3314088,3700297,3700429,3700440,3700489,4029815,4031109,4038214,4038394,4041776,4043492,4045096,4045293,4045840,4047140,4047454,4048347,4
4061666,4061980,4062724,4063220,4064468,4064796,4069829,4072270,4076997,4077580,4078588,4080760,4081039,4081164,4082230,4082441,4084250,
9,4097153,4097922,4097928,4098733,4098739,4099389,4102238,4103210,4103475,4103845,4104202,4104242,4104258,4104414,4106647,4109293
93,4115289,4115697,4116724,4116730,4116926,4116934,4117328,4117980,4118227,4118302,4118798,4119032,4119034,4119036,4120415,4120660,412091
045,4124090,4124139,4124850,4125837,4126203,4127095,4127445,4127744,4127775,4129520,4129555,4129559,4129633,4130408,4130411,4130560,41310
1420,4132528,4132952,4133090,4133114,4133121,4133125,4133245,4133274,4133416,4133434,4133799,4134062,4134265,4134440,4134561,4134919,4134
95576,4135744,4135856,4135934,4135953,4136220,4136235,4136458,4136546,4136627,4137110,4137128,4137461,4137462,4137545,4137597,4138341,413
139646,4140032,4140117,4140242,4140410,4140782,4140986,4141142,4141153,4141437,4141276,4141736,4141783,4141785,4141799,10200083,10202524,
9002245,19002249,19002252,19002257,19002548,19002664,19002671,19002880,19003319,19003321,19003323,19003407,19003408,19003409,19004006,190
9129,19004130,19004159,41317155',authuser:0,kscs:'efe7c74f_S88FWsSKMYeaU87bksAK',u:'efe7c74f',kGL:'GB'};google.kHL='en-GB';})();(function
google.li=0;google.getEI=function(a){for(var b;a&&(!a.getAttribute||!(b=a.getAttribute("eid")));)a=a.parentNode;return b||google.kEI};goo
.getAttribute||!(b=a.getAttribute("leid")));)a=a.parentNode;return b};google.https=function(){return"https:"==window.location.protocol};g
l};google.wl=function(a,b){try{google.ml(Error(a),!1,b)}catch(d){}};google.time=function(){return(new Date).getTime()};google.log=functio
new Image;var e=google.lc,f=google.li;e[f]=b;b.onerror=b.onload=b.onabort=function(){delete
l};google.vel&&google.vel.lu&&google.vel.lu(a);b.src=a;google.li=f+1}};google.logUrl=function(a,b,d,c,g){var e="",f=google.ls||"";d||-1!=
&ei="+google.getEI(c),-1==b.search("&lei=")&&(c=google.getLEI(c))&&(e+="&lei="+c));c="";!d&&google.cshid&&-1==b.search("&cshid=")&&(c="&
"gen_204")+"?atyp=i&ct="+a+"&cad="+b+e+f+"&zx="+google.time()+c;/^http:/i.test(a)&&google.ml(Error("a"),!1,{src:a,glmm:
nction(){google.y={};google.x=function(a,b){if(a)var c=a.id;else{do c=Math.random();while(google.y[c])}google.y[c]=[a,b];return!1};google
ogle.lm.push.apply(google.lm,a)};google.lq=[];google.load=function(a,b,c){google.lq.push([[a],b,c])};google.loadAll=function(a,b){google.
nction(){google.hs={h:true};})();(function(){google.c={c:{a:true,d:true,e:true,i:false,m:true,n:false}};google.sn='webhp';(function(){var
nction(a,b,c){a.addEventListener?a.removeEventListener(b,c,!1):a.attachEvent&&a.detachEvent("on"+b,c)},h=function(a,b,c){g.push({g:a,h:b
ddEventListener(b,c,!1):a.attachEvent&&a.attachEvent("on"+b,c)},g=[];google.timers={};google.startTick=function(a,b){var c=b&&google.time
le.timers[b].t.start:google.time();google.timers[a]={t:{start:c},e:{},m:{}};(c=window.performance)&&c.now&&(google.timers[a].wsrt=Math.f
ogle.timers[a]||google.startTick(a);c=void 0!==c?c:google.time();b instanceof Array||(b=[b]);for(var d=0;d<b.length;++d)google.timers[a].
r:b[d],ts:c}};google.c.e=function(a,b,c){google.timers[a].e[b]=c};google.c.b=function(a){var b=google.timers.load.m;b[a]&&google.wl("ch_m
· b=google.timers.load.m;if(b[a]){b[a]=!1;for(a in b)if(b[a])return;google.csiReport()}else google.wl("ch_mnb",{m:a})};google.rll=functio
});f(a,"load",d);f(a,"error",d);h(a,"load",d);b&&h(a,"error",d)};google.ull=function(){for(var a;a=g.shift();){f(a,g,a.h,a.l)};google.iTi
ogle.time();google.tick("load",e,b);a=a.id||a.src||a.name;google.timers.iml||google.startTick("iml");google.timers.iml.t[a]=b;google.c.c
```

Above: At first glance, some codes look like gobbledygook, but once you understand the language you can create files and programs.

WHY CODE?

When it comes to websites, hand-coding gives you far more control. No matter how good web development programs such as Dreamweaver or BlueGriffon are, being able to code a website from scratch brings with it many benefits for the web designer. Here are just a few:

- **Freedom**: WYSIWYG text editors and other web design platforms are always limited in their features. Coding allows you the freedom to do what you want.

- **Efficiency**: Having full control over the underlying code of a website means you can ensure it is optimized for search engines and is without superfluous code.

- **Maintenance**: If you learn how to use code, you can make changes and updates to websites simply and easily.

- **Consistency**: By coding you can ensure every element in your website is in the right place, so banners, images and menu items are all exactly where you want them.

```
<!DOCTYPE html>
<html>
<!-- created 2010-01-01 -->
<head>
  <title>sample</title>
</head>
<body>
```

Above: HTML is one of the most widely used coding languages in computing.

Hot Tip

A great way to practise coding is to copy the HTML source of a web page and make changes, which you can then view in your web browser and compare with the original.

Other Reasons to Code

If you have never learned to code and really want to, HTML, JavaScript and CSS are good places to start. In general, codes used to design websites are easy to learn. If you know some HTML or other web code, coding your own website is a great way to take advantage and improve your existing computer skills.

LEARNING TO CODE

This is not a book designed to teach you how to code. There is simply not enough space to cover the intricacies of HTML, JavaScript, CSS and the rest. However, there's no shortage of resources on the Web to help you learn to code. No matter what the language, you can find various communities and learning resources.

⟳   **Codecademy**: www.codecademy.com. One of the most popular places to learn to code. It is free to sign up and the platform's interactive learning makes it easy to develop as a web coder.

Below: Codecademy.

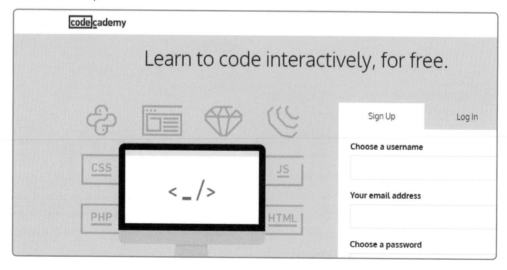

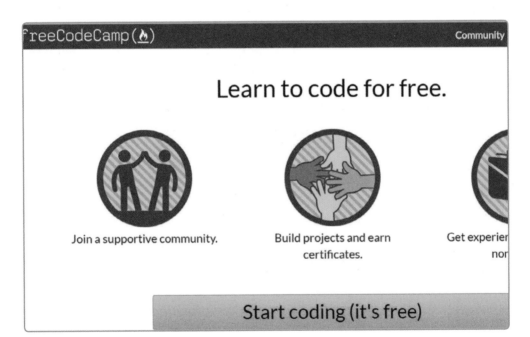

Codewars: www.codewars.com. More of a game than a learning resource, but you can develop coding skills by completing challenges.

Coursera: www.coursera.org. Large online library learning centre, taught by university professors.

FreeCodeCamp: www.freecodecamp.org. Provides a curriculum-based course and work experience coding for non-profit organizations.

Above: FreeCodeCamp.

W3Schools.com: www.w3schools.com. A great free resource from the World Wide Web Consortium – the body responsible for setting web standards – to learn a number of codes taking you from the basics right through to advanced coding.

Coding as a Career

Web code is a great introduction to coding in general. Many people who learn to code in HTML or other web languages soon find themselves hooked; some even become professional coders. Coding is a great skill to learn and useful in many fields beyond web design.

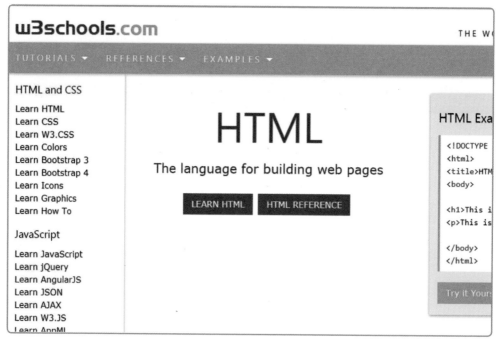

Above: W3schools.com

CODING TOOLS

The great thing about web coding is you do not need any specialist software or equipment. HTML code can be written out in a plain text file. You can get specialist software for this, but programs such as Microsoft Notepad and Notepad++ do just as well and the HTML files you create can be read by a regular web browser.

CODING HTML

As mentioned earlier in this book, HTML is a web language used to create the structure of a website. Code is written out into a text editor using HTML tags. The code also gives instructions as to the location, position and size of content. All text is held within the HTML document, while the code contains the location, size and position of multimedia such as images. When a web browser reads an HTML document, it creates the web page following the coded instructions.

Above: The HTML code for a website is contained in one or more HTML documents.

HTML Documents

An HTML document is just a text file with the .htm (.html) file extension. This tells a web browser that the file contains code, which it can use to create a web page. All HTML documents start with a document type declaration – `<!DOCTYPE html>` – then a series of tags is used to introduce content, create changes and structure the web page.

CODING JAVASCRIPT

At first glance, JavaScript looks a lot like HTML. JavaScript is designed to change the way browsers handle HTML content. Often it does specific tasks, such as change an image when a user clicks a button or accepts information

Jargon Buster

Programs and files that are on the host server are known as 'server-side'; files that operate on the host's machine are 'host-side'.

the user has typed in. JavaScript is a script not a code. While the terms are often synonymous, JavaScript frequently appears in short passages embedded within HTML documents.

```
<!DOCTYPE html>
<html>
<body>

<h2>JavaScript Statements</h2>

<p>JavaScript code blocks are written between { and }</p>

<button type="button" onclick="myFunction()">Click Me!</button>

<p id="demo1"></p>
<p id="demo2"></p>

<script>
function myFunction() {
    document.getElementById("demo1").innerHTML = "Hello Dolly!";
    document.getElementById("demo2").innerHTML = "How are you?";
```

Above: JavaScript often appears in short bursts of code, known as JavaScript statements, within HTML code.

Host-side

While HTML documents sit on a host server, JavaScript operates on a client's (user's) machine, allowing interactivity on the website. By sitting between the HTML document and the client's browser, JavaScript is able to make changes to the HTML code depending on what a user has inputted.

Hot Tip

Do not confuse JavaScript with Java. They are separate languages. JavaScript is a scripting language read by browsers only, while Java is used to create applications.

Writing JavaScript

Like HTML, JavaScript can be written in a text editor. It can even be embedded in an HTML document, although you can save JavaScript files separately by giving them the file extension .js and introduce them in the HTML code using the filename and file extension.

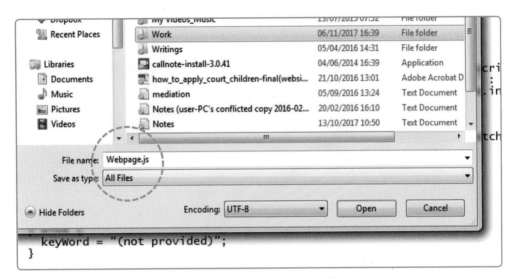

Above: JavaScript can be saved in a text document using the .js file extension.

CODING CSS

HTML was never designed to format web pages. Its original purpose was to describe how to display the content. While you use tags such as font and colour information on a website, if you want consistency, you have to add this to every page you code. CSS removes the need for style formatting in HTML and uses style sheets to tell a browser how a page should look.

CSS Files

CSS files can be written in a text editor, much like HTML, and saved with the .css file extension. You can link multiple HTML documents to the same .css file, so it can control the look and layout of every web page you create.

Right: CSS lets you set the structure of a web page using a style sheet that can be used by multiple pages.

```
/* begin: seaside-theme */

body {
    background-color:white;
    color:black;
    font-family:Arial,sans-serif;
    margin: 0 4px 0 0;
    border: 12px solid;
}
```

NUTS & BOLTS OF WEBSITE DESIGN

BASIC PRINCIPLES

It is essential to understand a few basic principles before you start on your web design, not just about how the pages should look, but also the implications of choosing certain styles and formats.

ALWAYS REMEMBER

Designers learning Internet skills should remember these pointers to good web design.

→ **Do not reinvent the wheel:** Have a good browse around the Web and, when you find a site layout you like, view its source code to see how it is constructed. Have a look at standard templates and themes, and see how those websites are constructed.

→ **Sketch out your design:** Get your design finalized in your mind by sketching it out. Know what buttons and links you want on each page and what pages they take you to. Be consistent, have a basic template for page headers, banners and standard information such as contact details that you want to appear on every page.

→ **Be strict with colours:** Select a scheme of complementary colours before you begin and do not stray from these colours.

Even changing colours slightly for different site sections is inadvisable, as readers might think they have been sent to an external site.

⊙ **Be efficient:** When considering things such as colour palettes and image resolution, go low, for example 800 x 600-pixel screen size and a 216-colour web-safe palette instead of higher-resolutions and too many colours, which could cause problems on low-specification machines.

⊙ **Keep file sizes small:** Larger graphics and lengthy pages with lots of multimedia take longer to load and could prompt users to click back. Compress image files as much as possible.

⊙ **Test your site:** Do this as your readers might see it, running it across as many browsers as possible on both Macs and Windows PCs and, if possible, on a range of mobile phones to check its universality.

Hot Tip

Most websites have a page header and a page footer. These are banners that run along the top and bottom on most web pages. Headers and footers are good places for company names, contact details and other permanent information.

Above: Websites contain various elements including menus, images, text and headers.

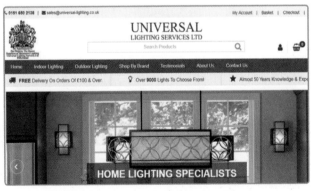

Above: Websites should be neatly structured, easy to navigate and eye-catching.

WEB CONVENTIONS

Certain conventions and ways of doing things have developed as the World Wide Web has evolved. Have a look at the way other websites do things. Often you will see similarities between websites in the way they are constructed and structured. Some of these conventions change over time but others have been around since the early days of the Web, such as most websites having a homepage or links being blue.

Homepage

Having a simple, easy-to-navigate website with a homepage that is easily accessible from all pages is important. You can do this with either a home icon or a link in the header or banner that takes you back to the homepage. Well-ordered directories or categories are also important so people can find the information they want on your website quickly and easily.

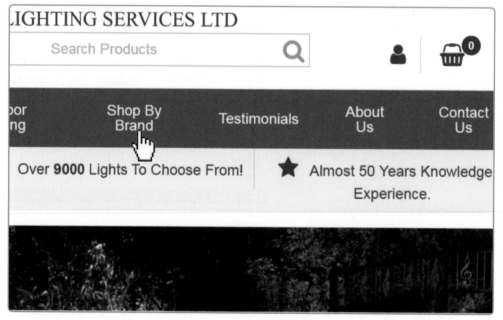

Above: Visitors need to be able to find what they are looking for, so websites need to be easy to navigate.

STAGE BY STAGE

A website can take some time to get from the drawing board to the Internet, but the process can be made a lot easier by taking it one stage at a time.

Purpose

Decide who your website is aimed at and what subject matter it will contain. Search the Web for similar sites and decide how yours will stand out. These decisions will help decide the tone of the site's overall design.

Layout

How many pages do you want? What are the main sections of your website? Draw up a list of the primary sections and subdirectories that the site will be split into. Create a storyboard – a flowchart showing how the pages will connect to the parent pages and each other.

	A	B	C	D
1				
2				
3				
4				
5		**Product Category 1**	**Product 1**	
6	**Homepage**		**Product 2**	
7			**Product 3**	
8				
9		**Product Category 2**	**Product 1**	
10			**Product 2**	
11			**Product 3**	
12		**Contact Form**		
13				
14		**About Us**		
15				
16		**Cart**		

Sheet1

Above: You can plan out how many pages you need and which pages they connect to on a spreadsheet.

Content

Decide on how much information you want to include. If it is written out, what is the word count? Bear in mind readers are reluctant to scroll down for more than one and a half screens, so run longer text on to a second page rather than force users to scroll away from the page header and navigation bar. Select what images and other media you want to include on your website.

THEME

The theme is the basic look of a website and will depend on the site's focus and target audience. If it is a business site, choose formal styles, serif fonts and cool shades; hobbyist or personal sites might go for a lighter feel with brighter colours and more informal typefaces.

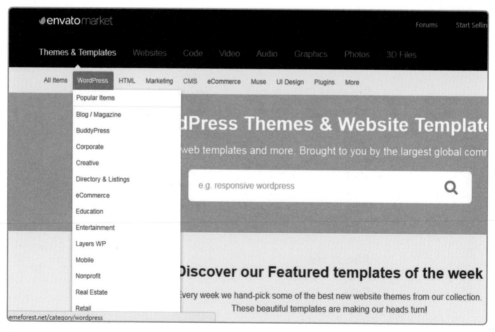

Above: Website templates are often sold by 'theme' so opt for the one that most closely suits your needs.

USABILITY

Have you ever visited a website looking for something in particular only to click away in frustration? Websites need to be usable and that means ensuring you have a good structure and layout.

STRUCTURING A WEBSITE

Readers need to be able to go from one page to another to find what they need, easily. Structuring a website is more than just adding links to pages. You need to structure your website's content too.

Directories

When a website loads, it does so by means of passing folders containing the content to the web browser. The more folders and information it has to pass, the more slowly the page will load. To ensure you only pass information that is needed or relevant, you can structure a website in directories.

Name	Date modified	Type	Size
8 techniques to practise mental toughne...	10/11/2017 12:37	File folder	
8 techniques to practise men			
api.js.download			
cb=gapi(1).loaded_0			
cb=gapi.loaded_0	07/11/2017 12:47	LOADED_0 File	
celebrating-pad-thai-5712000859504640-s	07/11/2017 12:47	PNG image	
dn.js.download	07/11/2017 12:47	DOWNLOAD File	
loading_24	07/11/2017 12:47	GIF image	
rs=AA2YrTuOvQ_qIcpji0vB5LaYqxDICKj-_A	07/11/2017 12:47	File	

8 techniques to practise mental toughness - CGMA Magazine_files
Date created: 10/11/2017 12:36
Size: 455 KB
Files: 1701260325001_5349323640001_5349286876001-th, ...

Above: File size of web folders is all important when it comes to page-loading speed.

Hot Tip

It is a good idea to decide the size of your website before figuring out its structure. With small sites, you may want all your information in one root directory, but for a larger site, you may want to use a directory system.

Root Directory

Directories are just folders. Each directory contains information relating to a specific topic or web page. The root directory is the first folder a browser will load; this will be all the content visible when somebody visits your homepage, so all the banners, text and images on this page are contained in this folder.

Above: The root directory contains all the standard elements you may need on your website.

Other directories and sub-directories below the root directory contain the content for other web pages. Because some of the information is shared among web pages, such as the header, footer and layout, you can keep this information in the root directory so subsequent web pages do not need to load this information when a user clicks on them.

File Organization

Before you start building the pages that will make up your website, decide how you want to store their constituent HTML and image files on the server. If a website consists of fewer than 20 pages, you can safely put them all in one top-level directory. To preserve order on larger sites, files can be divided into directories based on the site's menu structure. If your site is particularly complex, you can create further subdirectories. Each directory should have an index page (index.htm or equivalent).

Create a separate directory for images at the top level to ease management. Other resources, like Flash animations or movie files, should also be assigned a separate directory.

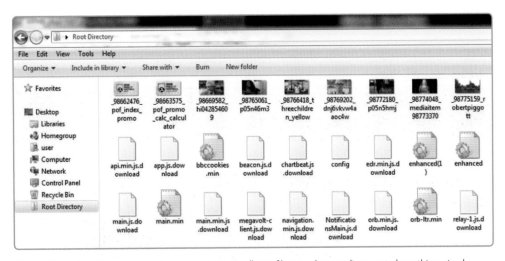

Above: If you do not have many web pages, you can put all your files into the root directory to keep things simple.

Types of Directory Structures

Hierarchical structure: A series of directories stem from the index page in the root directory. The index or homepage links to section pages, which link to a set of topic pages or third-level directories. Every page links to its parent and child page.

→ **Sequential structure**: Pages flow out from the homepage to form a linear structure. The navigation structure of each page merely takes the reader to 'Previous' and 'Next' pages, as well as back to the homepage.

Jargon Buster
Web pages that link to pages lower down in the directory system are known as 'parent pages', and the pages they link to as 'child pages'. Pages that are not linked to anything are known as 'orphan pages'.

→ **Grid structure**: All pages have equal weight and all link to each other. The user can follow any route through the pages, so the content of such a structure has to be well conceived so that each page stands independent of the others.

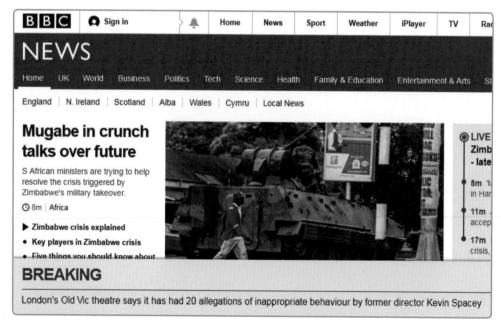

Above: All homepages are 'parent pages'. The pages they connect to in a website are its 'child pages'.

NAVIGATION

The purpose of a good structure is to make a website easy to navigate for its users. It entails identifying the content available and giving it a shape, starting with the homepage, where there is a choice of sections, from which you can select further subsections. It could also be linear, such as a company history where pages are viewed in a set order.

Hot Tip

When you have decided on a structure, sketch a storyboard showing the links between directories and pages and base your site and navigation system around it. A firm structure is the first step towards offering readers an intuitive, usable website.

Above: A useful feature on many websites is that when you click the header or company logo you are taken back to the homepage.

One of the complications of the Web is that not all users start at the same place. If they are clicking a link from another site or a search engine, they can enter your site at any point and not just the homepage.

Signposting

Every page needs navigational elements to take users around the site. These elements should look like navigational tools, in other words buttons should be labelled clearly to show what they are ('Home', 'Products', 'Shop' and so on). It is also a good idea to link to the homepage from every page on your site.

Navigational Aids

You need to ensure that pages that you want to be able to access from anywhere – such as the search box or a help file – are easy to find. Usually, these can form part of the navigation bar. This will typically be at the top of the page and is often set in a frame so it is always available. It may also be along the side or bottom of a page or you can opt for navigational tabs for each section.

Above: Navigational aids such as menu buttons help users find what they are looking for.

LAYOUT

Web page layout has come a long way from the early days, when each element lined up left in the window, one under another. Today, it can be an immense multimedia experience that, at its best, can rival TV.

Consistency

The important thing to remember in laying out your website and its separate pages is to be consistent. All web pages should resemble one another in general layout and structure. This means that all the elements, such as headers, footers, banners, sidebars, are all in the same place, and all pages share the same colours, themes and styles.

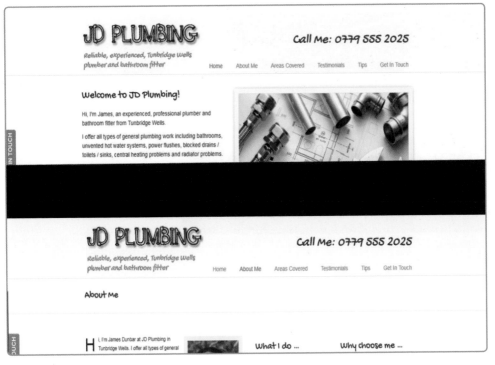

Above: Using the same header on all pages, as on this plumber's website, can create consistency.

Avoid Clutter

Your web page layout should look neat and uncluttered. Make use of sidebars and headers and menus. Make good use of categories and other ways of structuring the content on your website.

Search

An index used to be a crucial tool for web surfers looking for relevant information on a website. This is a list of all your web pages and how they connect to one another. Search engines still rely on an index to navigate your website and you can create xml sitemaps to help search bots index your pages and their links, but for human visitors, the best way to ensure easy navigation through your website is a search tool. Do not worry, you do not need to know any complicated HTML to install one on a website, as plenty of plug-ins and ready-made scripts are available.

Above: Search tools can make navigation easy.

Style Sheets

HTML's table tags and cascading style sheets (CSS) have added tools for creating grids that can lay out objects. Style sheets mean designers also have more control over the look and feel of a page. Style sheets provide a centrally stored set of rules for layout attributes, such as text size, line spacing or indents. A style sheet can be applied site-wide, so changes can be done in one hit rather than having to be applied to every instance.

Using CSS

As a layout tool, CSS treats each element as an object, or box. So, you can tell the browser the exact place on the screen you want the box placed. This can either be a pixel-precise co-ordinate (absolute) or relative to some other box or the top left of the browser (relative) so you can ensure elements are in the same place for every web page.

```
div.fixed {
    position: fixed;
    bottom: 0;
    right: 0;
    width: 300px;
    border: 3px solid #73AD21;
}
```

Above: With CSS you can fix positions of elements or place them relative to another object.

VIEWPOINT

Not everybody will view your website on a computer. In fact, more people access the Web on smartphones and tablets than on computers and laptops. The viewpoint is the visible area of a website. It may well be somebody is reading your website on a 3-inch screen, or they may have a 32-inch monitor. Obviously, you cannot fit the same amount of information on screens that vary so much in size.

Screen Friendly

Web designers used to fix the size of their web pages, so they knew all the information they wanted would appear when the page loaded. This is no longer always possible because of the number of devices on which people use the Internet.

Hot Tip

When adjusting a website for smaller devices, remember that people are used to scrolling vertically, not horizontally. Make sure your website is not too wide to fit into even the smallest screens when scaled.

Scaling

To fix the problem of varying screen size, modern browsers scale a web page so it fits the screen of the device that is accessing it. Of course, this could cause problems if the browser shrank everything, but you can tell the browser on a mobile device to move items as well, which often means coming up with multiple website structures for various sizes of device and adding these into CSS or HTML.

Above and Right: The same page (BBC homepage) appears differently on a mobile device compared to the desktop version.

READABILITY

Structure plays a key role in how readable a website is, but so does the type of font you use, the colours and the themes, as well as the actual content you are providing.

BEING READABLE

Have you ever visited a website and found it so difficult to read and unappealing that you clicked away? Maybe there were large chunks of text and no images, or the dreaded white text on a black background caused you to go dizzy as you tried to decipher the words. Perhaps the website just looked dull, uninspiring or downright ugly. Readability is as important as structure when it comes to providing web content.

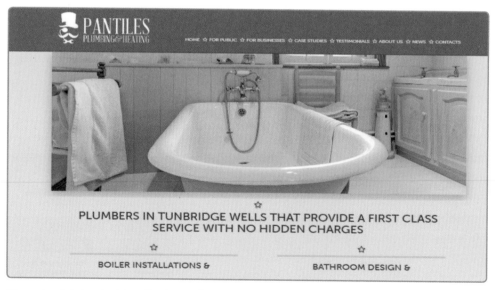

Above: A well-designed website will make use of images and colours, and contain readable content.

Content is King

It doesn't matter what font you use, how great-looking your website is and how cleanly it is structured if your content is poor. Good content means well-written information that your visitors will be interested in, as well as images and other multimedia to ensure your visitors have a positive experience.

TEXT

How text looks on a web page is important for readability. Long lines of text are difficult to read, so keep blocks of text short and narrow. Remember different people will be reading on different devices, so too much text may require lots of scrolling on a mobile device. A few other things can help with placing text:

Hot Tip

Spelling and grammar are as important as valid hyperlinks and image references. Always create content in a word processor and get someone else to proofread it before publication.

Above: Do not overburden the page with too much text. Keep things simple and to the point like this plumber's website has done.

➔ **Headings**: Use headers (html H tags, e.g. <h1>, <h2>) to break up your text with sub-headings.

➔ **Be simple**: Do not use too many typefaces on a page. Use one font for paragraph text and one for headings.

Jargon Buster

Fonts are the various styles of typeface you can use. These range from Comic Sans to Arial and Times New Roman.

➔ **Check alignment**: Left-align text only. Trying to justify text only leads to issues when scaling for smaller devices.

➔ **Make it easy on the eye**: Make sure the text contrasts with the background. Avoid light text on a dark colour.

Typography

Typography covers the way your typeface looks. Things such as font, size, style and colour of text are important to get right. How your type looks can affect how easy it is to read. If you are intending to use CSS when you design your website, you have more control over how your text will appear on another device. However, short of testing your website on every device imaginable, you have no guarantee how things are going to look. Keeping to good practice will ensure maximum readability of your text.

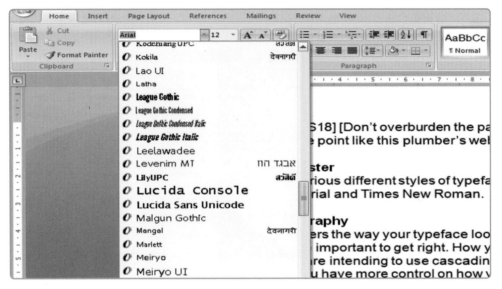

Above: We are all used to using fonts in word processors and other programs but you have to choose carefully for your website.

Good Typography Practice

→ **Sans-serif fonts**: Serifs are those little projections on letters you often see in print publications. Times New Roman is a serif font, while Arial is sans (without) serif. A good rule of thumb is that sans-serif fonts are easier to read on screen while serif fonts are better for print.

→ **Simple**: You can never be sure what fonts are installed on the device being used to browse your website. Choose the most common fonts or risk your content turning into gobbledygook.

→ **Upper and lower case**: Stick to capitalization conventions. Too many capitals can be off-putting to the reader.

→ **Styles**: Avoid cutting and pasting bold and italic fonts. If you want to style fonts, add the information into HTML or CSS or use your WYSIWYG editor to do it for you.

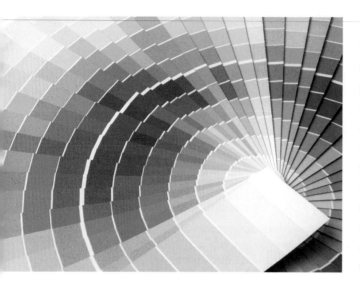

COLOUR

The colours and shapes you choose to use on your website can make it smart and impactful or send your viewer into a web of confusion, at best having trouble identifying your brand and at worst unable to follow your message. Choosing colour for a website is not as simple as just picking from a palette or colour wheel, as colours need to be specified in HTML, and that means they need a number.

Web Colours

Unlike in print where four colours – CMYK (cyan, magenta, yellow and black) – are merged in inks to create all the other colours, the Web uses the three-colour RGB concept, where every pixel on a computer screen is comprised of varying levels of red, green or blue light (RGB).

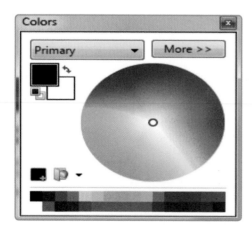

Left: A colour wheel.

Jargon Buster

Pixels are the tiny dots that make up an LCD or plasma screen and turn light into the text and images that you see on screen.

RGB Colour

You have to specify the amount of red, green and blue light that is projected on screen when choosing a colour for a web page. Thus a warm red would require a maximum red value of 255, and green and blue values of zero. However, colours within HTML pages or cascading style sheets (CSS) have to be specified not by their RGB values, but in hexadecimal code. You can find colour-code converters online.

Colour Wheels

A colour wheel gives designers a visual representation of the colours available to them. All graphics design packages let you access colour wheels to select a colour. Colour wheels usually come in both RGB and CMYK models, so you can be sure of finding web-friendly colours.

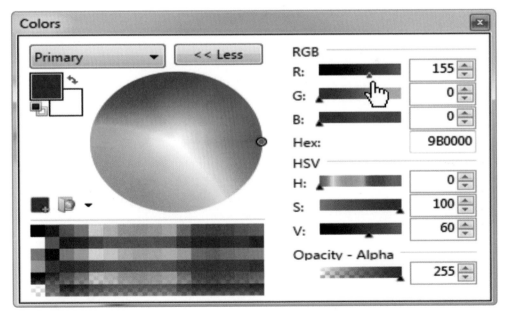

Above: RGB colour represents the amount of red, green or blue light that makes up the colour.

Hot Tip

Three colours that are equidistant on a wheel, or their tints, tones and shades, tend to work well together. When using a colour wheel, try to keep the hue, saturation and light settings consistent too.

COLOUR COMBINATIONS

Almost all printed documents use dark text on a white background. Just because the Web gives easy access to thousands of colours, do not try to use as many as you can all at once. You have to use sensible, legible colour combinations.

Contrast

When choosing a colour scheme for the text-heavy areas of your site, contrast is crucial. Black on white is the obvious choice, but if you want to add colour, dark blues, greens or reds make for legible text on white or light backgrounds. Combining dark and light shades of the same colour is a common solution. But, while they make good headline colours, resist the temptation to use bright colours for text, as this could prove hard to read for any length of time.

Mismatching Colours

Mismatching colours can result in a garish website. The eye is a good indicator of which colours complement each other and which clash, but you can get a fair idea by using a colour wheel. Think about colour warmth too. Try not to mix warm colours with cold colours.

Top Stories

Mugabe in crunch talks over his future
S African ministers are trying to help resolve the crisis triggered by Zimbabwe's military takeover.

🕐 8 minutes ago

Zimbabwe army takeover - latest

🕐 15 November 2017

Old Vic lists 20 allegations against Spacey

🕐 5 minutes ago

Above: Using dark text on a lighter background can help you highlight text, such as this boxout on the BBC website.

If you want a bold, brazen website, go for warm reds and yellows, while cooler hues of blue and green are more calm and soothing. Do not over-burden a page with too much colour. Keep a general theme with separate but complementary background colours for sidebars, boxouts, main text and headers.

Jargon Buster

Boxouts are boxes containing extra information, separate to the main body of text. Use a bold typeface to make the text stand out.

Above: Choose a colour palette that suits your website.

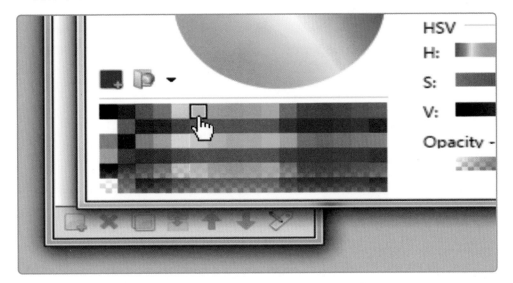

Above: Choose colours carefully as they are vital for setting the tone of your website.

IMAGES

Images are key to an impactful and successful website. It is therefore essential to understand which file formats are best for which types of image, and how to make sure you are sending the right messages with the images you include.

IMAGE TYPES

Image files contain all the information necessary to display an image in a browser or on image-handling software. Images come in various formats, each with its own advantages and disadvantages.

JPEG

By far the most common image file type, and the best file format for images with lots of subtle colours, is JPEG (named after the developers Joint Photographic Experts Group). JPEG images are compressed to reduce the file sizes and shorten download time, but there is a trade-off; the more you compress a JPEG, the worse the image looks as the compression technique removes detail.

The file extension is .jpg or .jpeg.

FILE TYPES

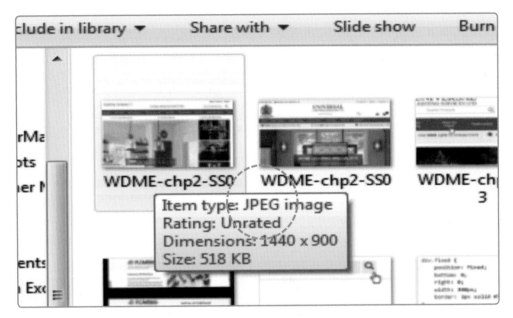

Above: JPEG images are the most widely used images on the Web.

PNG

The PNG (Portable Network Graphics, pronounced 'ping') format also compresses files but it does so more sparingly. While this leads to less loss of detail, it means PNG files are larger than JPEGs. It does have one distinct advantage, however: the PNG format can handle transparent backgrounds (JPEG images always convert transparency to white).

Above: The PNG format lets you create objects with transparent backgrounds, useful for placing images over other content, such as this pointer.

GIFs

The Graphics Interchange Format comes in two types:

→ **GIF**: GIF file sizes are larger than JPEG or PNG images. GIFs are best used for images with a few flat blocks of colour, such as logos or simple illustrations.

➔ **Animated GIF**: Combines images into a single GIF file to create an animation. The compact GIF file can be put on your web page like any other graphics file.

Hot Tip

You can create animated GIFs using online platforms such as giphy.com and gifmaker.me.

Non-Compressed Formats

There are numerous other image file formats but some are unsuitable for web use because of their size. TIFF (Tag Image File Format), for instance, is one of the most widely used file formats for images, particularly in the print world, as it is cross-platform and supported on many operating systems, including Windows, UNIX and Macintosh. Files in the TIFF format

have .tif as the extension but its file sizes make it inappropriate for web use. However, TIFF images and other unsuitable image files can be converted to JPEGs and other file formats using image manipulation software.

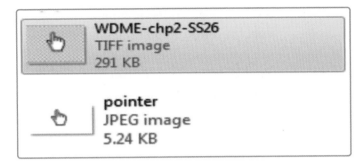

Above: TIFF files are much larger than the same image saved as a PNG or JPEG format.

IMAGE MANIPULATION

With the power of web-graphics editors, a basic image does not need to stay basic for long. It can be significantly improved by a relatively simple addition, such as a coloured border, cropping or altering the colours of the image. This software can also change file formats on images and resize them. Image manipulation software varies from the simple and inexpensive to the sophisticated and pricey.

↪ **Adobe Photoshop:** The king of image software. With the most features, this image software is the choice of professionals and comes with Adobe Creative Suite.

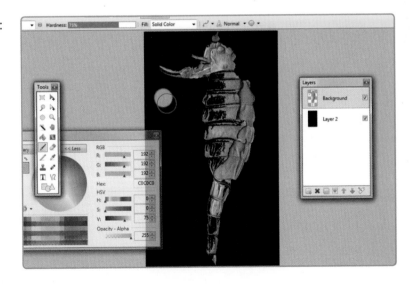

Right: Image manipulation software lets you resize, change format and touch up images.

➔ **Microsoft Paint**: Available on most PCs, simple programs like Paint let you crop, resize and change the file format of images.

➔ **Gimp**: Often described as 'a free Photoshop', Gimp is open-source and packed with nearly as many features as Adobe's software and is available for free.

Improving Images

Image manipulation software offers you a number of tools that enable you to gloss over any faults on the image. Using the Clone brush, you can copy (clone) from one part of an image to another to cover any flaw in the background. A Retouch tool enables you to apply special effects to a section of an image rather than to the entire graphic. It is useful if you want to lighten colours or emboss a part of the image.

Below: You can use all sorts of tools to make changes to images.

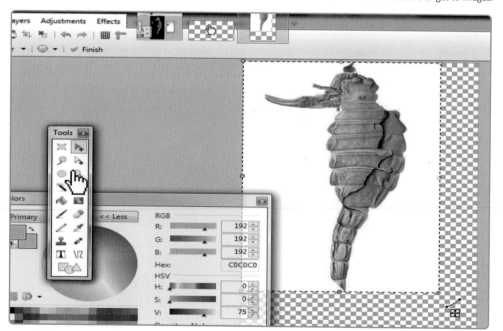

You can alter the orientation of an image by flipping it (reversing an image along its vertical axis) or mirroring it; that is, reversing it horizontally so that what was on the left side becomes the right and what was on the right appears on the left.

CACHING IMAGES

In the battle to minimize download time, the browser cache stores images to the visitor's hard drive or memory so that, if they are needed again, they can be displayed pretty much instantly. As a result, icons or navigation bars cost nothing in download time after the first use. The cache can also be used to preload large images files and store them until they need to be displayed.

IMAGE COPYRIGHT

When using images on a website, you need to make sure you have permission from whoever owns the copyright. Photo libraries provide images under licence, which you can use in different ways. Some provide restrictions, others let you use images freely, some charge royalties each time you use an image and others are royalty-free.

THINGS TO CONSIDER

You have your content, you have your images and you have worked out your structure. You may think you are ready to design your website, but you may need to consider a few other things first.

BEING FOUND

There is no point going to all the effort of designing a website if nobody is going to see it. Who is your audience and how will they find you? Unless you can give every visitor your specific URL, how are people going to know your website exists and how to find it? The primary way people find most websites these days is by using a search engine, so your website needs to be indexed.

Luxury Lighting: Lighting Shops UK | Home Lighting | Exterior Lights
https://www.luxurylighting.co.uk/ ▾
As specialist **lighting** shops are few and far between, we have customers visit our showroom from the surrounding towns of **Maidstone**, Rochester, Ashford, ...
Contact Us · Kitchen Ceiling Lights · Jenny Worrall Table Lamps · Exterior Lighting

Lighting Product Retailers in Maidstone | Reviews - Yell
https://www.yell.com › Maidstone › Lighting Product Retailers ▾
Find **Lighting** Product Retailers in **Maidstone**, with business contact details, opening hours and reviews. ... Shortlist More info for The Wall **Lighting Company** Ltd.

Event Lighting Hire & Audio Visual Equipment, Kent, London, STL ...
www.stlproductiongroup.co.uk/ ▾
Kent based event **lighting**, rigging, sound and production services for London UK ... **Lighting**, power and audio visual equipment for hire. ... **Company Name**:.

Kent Electrical & Lighting Centre
www.kent-lighting.co.uk/ ▾
Shop powered by PrestaShop.

Maidstone Branch | TLC Electrical - TLC Electrical Supplies
https://www.tlc-direct.co.uk/Information/branches/MD.html ▾
Maidstone Branch. **Maidstone** Branch ... Email. sales@tlc-direct.co.uk ... Towns: Ashford, Aylesford, Bearsted, **Maidstone**, Otford, Sevenoaks, West Malling ...

Above: If you do not appear on a search engine how will people find you?

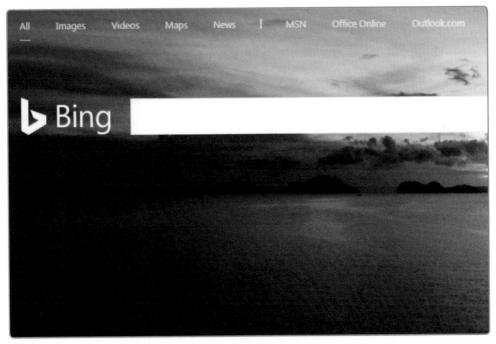

All   Images   Videos   Maps   News | MSN   Office Online   Outlook.com

Above: Search engines like Google and Bing need to index your site so that search results can be shown.

Search Engines

Search engines such as Google and Bing return a list of sites based on the words typed into the search box. If you want your site to be noticed, it is important you ensure search engines can find you. Most search engines work by sending out a spider that crawls the web to find as many pages as possible, which are then indexed and categorized. Consequently, you can improve the chances of your site being returned on a relevant search by filling in the information in the meta tags.

Jargon Buster

Used by search engines for indexing web pages, meta tags are hidden HTML tags that contain snippets of information such as the website's description and associated keywords.

SEARCH ENGINE OPTIMIZATION

Search engine traffic comes in two forms:

➔ **Paid for:** Search engines host pay-per-click advertising, usually at the top of their results page. Adverts are related to keyword searches.

➔ **Organic:** Non-paid-for searches are displayed in order of relevance to the search request.

Ranking

In order to appear high in the search rankings, your website needs to be optimized. Search engine optimization (SEO) ensures your website is easily found by search engines and they can easily ascertain what your website is about. With so many other websites out there, the more information you provide the higher in the rankings you will appear. Since people rarely

Hot Tip

Search engines ascertain a website's relevance based on factors such as how related the information contained in the web page is to the search request, how popular it is and what other websites link to it.

click past the first page of search results, and often rarely past the first few results, the higher you are in the rankings, the better.

Importance of SEO

➔ **Keywords**: Using words relating to your website, such as 'plumber', 'repair', 'emergency', helps search engines match it to search requests.

Above: Pay-per-click adverts often appear at the top of search results, and in Google's case are marked with an 'Ad' symbol.

➔ **Meta tags**: A good description, title and keywords in your meta tags help provide search engines with important information about your website.

➔ **Structure**: Spiders need to crawl the content easily, which means navigating from page to page.

➔ **Speed**: Slow websites may be penalized in search engine rankings.

➔ **Links**: How many people link to your website, and who they are, helps establish authority and popularity. Who you link to can also have an effect.

Above: You will see the meta description in search results. This text does not appear on the actual website.

BASIC WEBSITE DESIGN

GETTING STARTED

Keeping it simple and using a template or an online web designer have plenty of advantages. You can have a fully functional website up and running in no time without compromising its quality.

CHOOSING YOUR TOOLS

If you have made the choice to design your own website, using a template and an online WYSIWYG design program can be the simplest solution, but there are still more choices to be made. Choosing the wrong template can mean having to go right back to the start. You need a good checklist of what you do and do not need:

Above: Using a template can mean you have the basics for your website already done.

Cart: Do you need a way for customers to make purchases?

Blog: Do you need a blog as well as a website?

Adverts: Are you happy to run third-party advertising on your website, or do you want to run your own adverts?

Content: Do you need to host a lot of large files on your website or have dozens of different pages?

WHAT YOU WILL NEED

What you will need before you start will depend on what your plans are for designing your website. You may want to use a pre-existing template on a web host's design platform, or you may want to use a template from a third-party source, make changes to it, and then upload

Above: A template is essentially a ready-built website that you can customize.

it to your server yourself, or you may not want to use a template at all and do it all from scratch. At the very least you will have some sort of plan of your website, what you want included, what the content is and its basic structure.

Hot Tip

The great advantage to a template is that they already have placeholders for various elements such as images, links, body text, banners and headers, which you can move around, remove or add to.

TEMPLATES

Website templates are pretty flexible so you can take out anything you do not want, add in what you do want and make a website that suits your needs. How much you change a web template is up to you, as is the type of template you use. When selecting a template you have three choices:

Above: To begin designing your website can be as easy as signing up and clicking 'Edit' next to the template you want to adapt.

 **Design platform**: If you are using design software provided by your web host or other online portal, they will have a selection of templates to choose from.

 **Third party**: You can find an almost unlimited choice of website templates online that you can use to build your website then upload to your host.

 **Create your own**: You can create your own website template on web design software.

Template Theme

You won't struggle to find website templates, but you do need to be specific in your search for themes. Templates are offered ordered in business or website types, so if you have a business in a particular field, such as IT, opt for a theme in that category.

DOWNLOADING A TEMPLATE

If you choose to use a third-party template, you will need to download it to your desktop before you can use it or upload it to your web server.

1. Find the template you want to use and click the download button.

Hot Tip

Some web-hosted design platforms won't let you build a website without a template, so if you want to start from scratch, you can delete all the elements and pages in a template and begin with a blank page.

2. Your website files will normally be compressed, so use software such as WinRAR or WinZip to uncompress them.

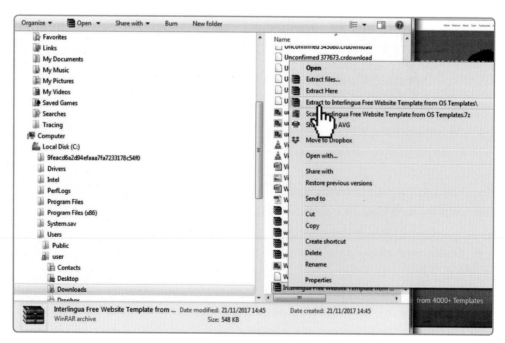

Above: You will have to extract your compressed website template files into a folder.

3.   You should have a folder containing all the files of your website template.

Choosing your Editing Tool

Once you have your template, you are going to want to change the text, add additional pages, move things around and make changes to the layout and colours, but to do this you can either dive into the HTML and website files, making changes to the code and adding content directly to your web folders, or you can choose a WYSIWYG editor such as Dreamweaver (more on this in the next section).

It is far easier, of course, to use the templates provided by your web host, where you can simply click on 'Edit' in one of their templates and begin making changes.

Above: Wix's web design editor.

What Do You Need?

All web development tools vary. Some provide extensive functionality, while some online tools may only let you tweak templates and drag and drop content, in which case you need to make sure your plans match up with your ability to make changes to the template. For instance, if the template allows for only a maximum of six menu items, but you have seven product categories for which you want to create pages, you may have to find another template.

The critical thing to remember when using a template is to ensure it has all the elements you need:

⊖ **Pages**: How many web pages does the site need to contain?

⊖ **Content**: Will the template accommodate all your content, words and pictures?

⊖ **Header**: Can you ensure the header matches your business colours and can include your logo?

⊖ **Menu**: Can you edit the menu items to the name and number you need?

⊖ **Images**: Is there a place for a background image or image to accompany text?

Left: Check all the pages have all the elements and placeholders you need.

EDITING YOUR TEMPLATE

While a template may give you the basic themes and structure for your website, you will need to add your content and personalize it.

EDITING TOOLS

All editing tools vary. There is simply not space in this book to explore how they all work, but to make basic changes to a website template most editors will let you alter the following:

→ **Web pages:** You can add and remove web pages and link them all into your preferred parent-and-child structure.

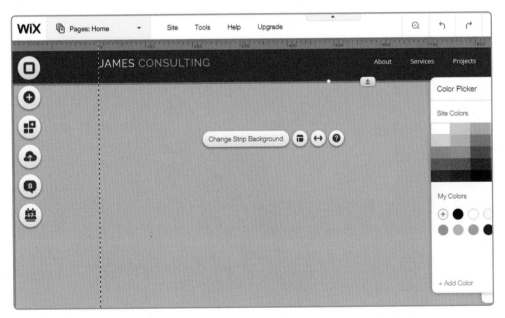

Above: You should be able to change most things on your template, from colours to images and text.

Elements: Menus, headers, sidebars and images can usually be altered and moved.

Content: Text can be uploaded and changed. You will also be able to upload images and other content.

Interactivity: Carts, social network connections and contact forms can sometimes be added.

Style: You can change the colours and fonts to alter the look and feel of a website.

CREATING YOUR STRUCTURE

While your website template may contain a basic structure, you can make changes to include the pages and content that you need. You can do this by adding or taking away pages and linking them to the main menu so they can be easily found.

Step 1. Clicking Pages in Wix.

ADDING PAGES IN WIX.COM

Adding and changing pages in a website editor such as Wix is usually straightforward.

1. Click the page edit menu item. On Wix it is called Pages and is in the top left corner.

2. Note that each page corresponds to a menu item.

3.   Click the edit button (3 dots) on any page you want to rename or remove. In this menu, you can also duplicate pages.

4.   Click "+ Add Page" to add a page and rename.

Step 3. You can rename, delete, duplicate or add a new page.

ADDING AND REMOVING ELEMENTS

Web pages contain all sorts of elements. Your template too will have a number of placeholders for elements, so you will have to decide what you need. Elements may include images, text boxes, headers, sidebars, social media buttons, menu buttons, and many more. Usually these can be easily added and removed using the web designer's menu systems.

Moving Elements

Online web tools make it easy to add and remove different elements. If you have ever created a blog, you will have some idea. Elements (such as text box or an image) can be clicked on, and you simply drag and drop elements wherever you want them on the page.

Hot Tip

If you want to create a child page to connect parent pages, this can often be done on an online web development tool, using the add subpage function.

Above: Elements are easily moved or removed.

CHANGING YOUR HEADER

One of the most important elements to get right is the header. The header usually sits on top of each web page and represents your company branding. Headers often include a business name and logo, and are often created to match a company's colours and style choices.

You may want to change a number of things in your header:

↪ **Title**: Headers usually have a title. This should be your business name.

↪ **Colour**: You may have company branding you want to match.

↪ **Imagery**: Logos and other images can be uploaded to your header.

↪ **Content**: If you want your contact details or other information in your header, this needs to be added.

Above: Headers sit at the top and may include such things as your company or business name.

Size and position: You may want a small header to the side or a long banner along the top.

CHANGING BACKGROUND COLOURS

If you do not like the background colours on your template, or you want to more closely match your business branding to the website, you can make colour changes. However, think about how complicated your web page is, and how many elements it contains. There may well be several background colours used on the page, some for the border, some for the main page, some for the background to other elements. Be prepared to make multiple changes.

Above: Changing the colour of headers or backgrounds is often very simple.

Text Changes

If you do not like the fonts and styles of text used on your template, this is also easily fixed, but you must take care to be consistent and use fonts sparingly and wisely.

PREVIEWING CHANGE

Online WYSIWYG editors are often obscured by menus and rulers so it can be difficult to make out what the changes actually look like. Fortunately, most platforms have a 'preview site' mode. This enables you to see your web page as it looks online and how people will see it when the website finally goes live.

Above: Preview mode lets you see how your website will look.

Mobile Editing

Your editor may even have a mobile version, so you can edit your website to look good on smaller screens. This can result in lots of structural changes, so it is important you see where all your content will be once you start adding it. Make sure you can navigate easily on all versions of your website.

INTELLIGENT DESIGN

If all this tweaking and tinkering with page layouts, structures and colours seems like too much hard work to you, you may find an even easier solution. Some web platforms now have intelligent software that will create a website for you based on you providing it with some basic information. Some of these website builders are quite impressive and will even create a website based on your company logo.

Using WIX ADI

One of the most impressive intelligent design platforms is WIX ADI.

1. Choose the type of website you want (for example business, education) at https://www.wix.com/new/site?

2. Click 'Start Now' when you see 'Let Wix ADI Create a Website for You'.

3. Answer or skip the questions it asks about the type of website you want.

OPTIONAL

Does your website need any of the following features?

☐ Sell online

☐ Take bookings & appointments

☐ Get subscribers

☐ Create a blog

Step 3. Answering questions about the sort of website you want.

Step 5. Wix will create the entire website, but you can still make changes if you do not like certain aspects.

Hot Tip

Some web builders have a handy zoom-out function that lets you see and edit all the elements on your web page at once rather than having to scroll up and down.

---

4. Click 'Start', choose a theme and the system will create your homepage based on the information provided.

5. You can choose another theme, adjust the one you are given, or accept the homepage that the system has created and then move on to subsequent pages.

GETTING IT RIGHT

No matter how you create your basic template and structure your website, you need to ensure you have got it right before you start adding content to your web pages. The last thing you want is to add all your text, images and other content, only to have to remove it all as you have realized you have missed a page out, have forgotten elements or need to change colours.

ADDING YOUR CONTENT

Once you have your basic template, it is time to start adding content to your website. This may mean text, images, videos as well as any other content that you want to share.

WEB CONTENT

Whether you just want people to know you are out there, or you want to convince somebody to contact you or buy your products, content is the whole point of a website. Your content needs to fit with both your audience and the purpose for which you have designed your website. Writing content for your website should not be rushed.

Copy

Even though a website can be as small or large as you like, you still need to write clean, crisp and concise copy. Some businesses pay large sums of money to ensure they have the best copy available, but if you have a good grasp of English it is possible to write it yourself.

Below: You can use a word processor to write your web copy and take advantage of the spell checker.

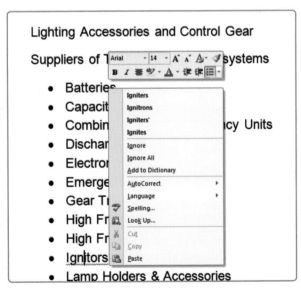

Jargon Buster

Copy is a term used in publishing and simply means the text of a document that will be published.

Tips to Writing Good Web Copy

The rules to writing good web copy are similar to those for writing for a printed publication:

- **Concise:** Do not use more words than necessary. Always keep to the point and explain your products or services using simple language.

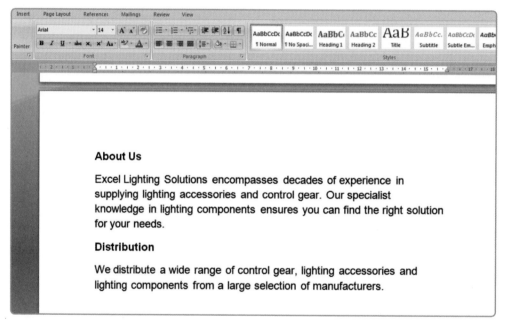

Above: Keep copy short and concise.

- **Bullets:** Use bullet points.

- **Headers:** Use headers to separate paragraphs.

- **Keep it short:** Paragraphs should be no more than four sentences and sentences no more than twelve or so words.

- **Jargon:** Be careful with technical terms. Will all your intended audience understand them?

- **Make it personal:** Use the first (I, us, we, my, ours) and second person (you, yours) when describing you and your customers.

When cutting and pasting text for use on the Web, paste the text in a plain text editor such as Notepad then cut and paste from that document to avoid transferring styles and formatting.

ADDING COPY

You can choose to add copy to your web template in a number of ways. The simplest way is to cut and paste it into a text box on your template. It should be noted, however, that cutting and pasting from word-processing programs such as MS Word can take some formatting and style information with it, which may not import well into the web editor you are using. It is always best to paste plain text, or type the copy into the text box itself.

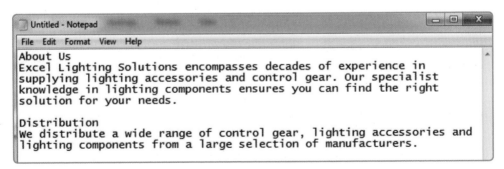

Above: It is always best to copy and paste plain text when designing your web pages.

UNDERSTANDING TEXT BOXES

Text boxes can be placed anywhere on a web page. Essentially, they are like an individual document. Once you have placed your text in a text box, you can move the whole box anywhere you want. You can also change the size and shape of a text box and adjust the font and style of all the text contained in it.

Justification

When pasting into a text box you can often choose the alignment of the text. You can generally align left, right, centred, or you can justify it (where both the left and right margins of the text are aligned). For web copy, it is always best to align either left or right, as any scaling could cause problems with justified text.

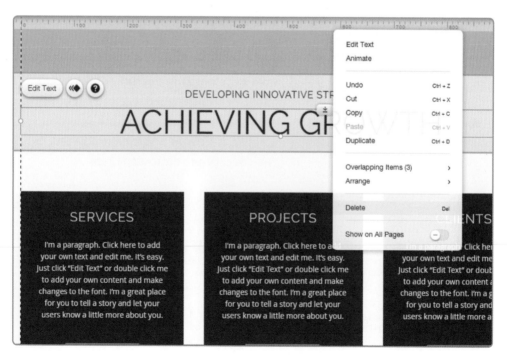

Above: It is easy to edit, delete, or replace text in a text box on a WYSIWYG editor.

Changing Styles and Fonts

You can normally change a number of attributes of the copy in your text box, including size, font and heading type. Remember, your web editor will be converting all the information into HTML for use on a browser. Because each text box is a web page element, it is best to keep the style and sizes of text in each box the same. In fact, when it comes to using text, it is best to be consistent in style with all your copy.

Hot Tip

Some web editors let you 'pin' an element to a web page. This means if you scroll down, the element will always stay in the same place; as such, pinned elements, such as navigation buttons and headers, should always be at the top.

Above: You can adjust font, font size, styles and other attributes of copy in a text box.

ADDING LINKS

Links are what make the Web go round. You can link internally, that is to other pages and sections of your website, or you can have external links on your website. External links come in two types:

- **Inbound links**: These are links on other websites that link to your web page. If it is a brand new website, you won't have any inbound links yet.

- **Outbound links**: These are links to other people's websites on your web pages. When a user clicks the link they are sent to the web page you have linked to.

> ## Hot Tip
>
> **If you are updating an existing website you may already have people linking to your content, so you need to make sure they are linking to the right page.**

Using Links

You need to be careful when using external links. The last thing you want to do is encourage people to leave your website, but links can be useful for pointing people to other resources they may find useful.

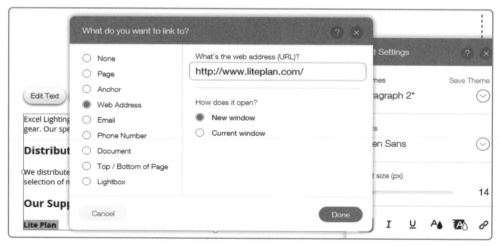

Above: If you add a URL, when a user clicks that anchor text they can be taken to that website.

Jargon Buster

When you turn text into a link, this is known as anchor text. Search engines regard anchor text in a similar way to keywords.

Left: Clicking the web symbol turns the text into 'anchor text'.

How to Add a Link

Using an online WYSIWYG editor, adding a link to your text, or even to an element, is very similar to adding a link to a word-processing document or email. Simply highlight the text you want to use to form the link, use the link symbol and put in the URL of the page to which you want to link. If you want to link internally, simply use your own web pages as the destination. Some web editors let you link to all sorts of internal website elements, such as particular anchor text on a web page.

ADDING IMAGES AND GRAPHICS

Few websites can get away with just text. Images are just as important for web pages as text and can be used for various reasons and in various elements on a website:

- **Header**: Logos and other images are often used in headers.

- **Highlight**: You can use an image to highlight a particular aspect of your content, such as to describe a product or service.

⊙ **Information:** A picture paints a thousand words and so images and graphics are a great way to explain things.

⊙ **Background image:** Using an image as a backdrop can work well on a website, but you need to be careful that the colours of an image do not obscure any text laid over the top.

Above: A background image can create an impact on a homepage.

Uploading Images

Images are very easily uploaded to a web design platform. If you want to use an image as a backdrop, you need to go into the background settings. This should let you choose an image to upload for use as a backdrop.

Images can also be uploaded into image boxes. Image boxes are similar to text boxes in that they turn the image into an element, but you can do other things to them, such as add a frame around the image or make the image linkable (so when you click the image it acts as a link).You may also be able to do some basic image manipulation on your web design editor, such as cropping the image, shrinking it or expanding it.

Hot Tip

When scaling an image, if you hold down the Shift key you can normally maintain the correct aspect ratio regardless of how large or small you make it.

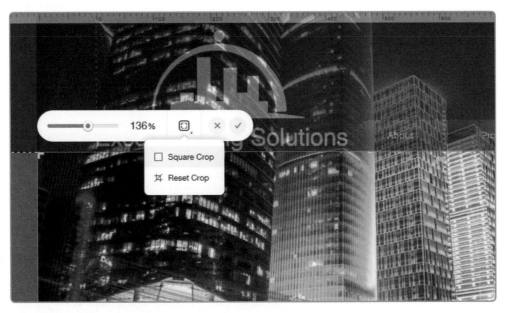

Above: You should be able to do some basic image editing such as cropping.

ADDING OTHER CONTENT

Depending on the web design tool you are using, you may also be able to add other types of content to your website, including:

- ➔ **Multimedia:** You can sometimes include videos, audio and other multimedia to a website but you should use them sparingly.

- ➔ **Files:** You can link to FTP files so people can download PDFs, brochures and other documents.

- ➔ **Functionality:** Contact forms, social media buttons and other elements can be added to your website.

- ➔ **Payment:** Your web designer may help you create a storefront or include a shopping cart and payment system.

Jargon Buster

File Transfer Protocol (FTP) is a web protocol that lets people download files from a server.

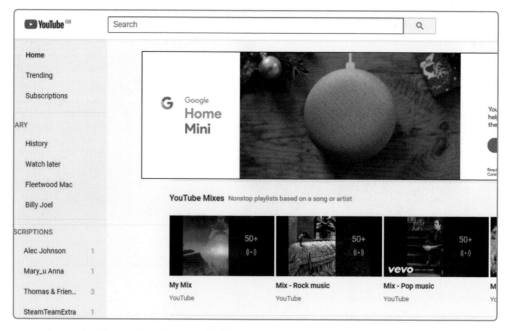

Above: You may be able to embed videos from YouTube or other channels.

TEST AND LAUNCH

**Once your basic website is designed, it's time to get it out there.
The first step is a thorough test before launch. Then it's all systems go!**

TESTING

The first area for testing, especially for designers, is the look and feel of a website. Check every page to make sure they are consistent in layout, colour and style. Check all the elements are in the right place on every web page. You then need to ensure all your navigational aids and links are working. Professional web designers take pains in testing their websites, often using third-party usability testers who perform sequences of pre-set tasks to make sure that a site's navigation and design is optimized.

Usability Testing

While your budget may not stretch to hiring third-party testers, you can still get a few friends or colleagues to look round the site before it goes live. Ask them to navigate their way to a certain page from the homepage. If they struggle, something as basic as the wording on your navigation menu could need changing.

UPLOADING A WEBSITE

Once finished, the website has to be published and made available to its audience, which means uploading the finished pages to your server. If you have used a web tool provided by your web host, this is often very straightforward; you just need to follow the on-screen instructions. Sometimes it can be as simple as clicking 'Publish' in the menu system.

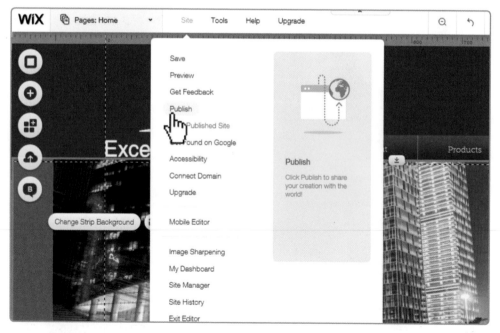

Above: Most web hosts make it easy to go live with your website, such as Wix, which you can publish straightaway on their domain.

Uploading Web Files

If you are uploading a website you created elsewhere, you will first need to save your website to your desktop then upload it to your server. There are a number of ways to do this.

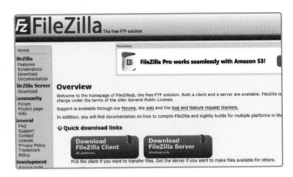

Above: Software such as FileZilla can help you transfer your website files to your host server.

- **Upload:** Your web host may have a simple uploading system where you can just upload your folders from your desktop.

- **FTP:** The traditional way to transfer web files was by FTP (File Transfer Protocol), but you can find software to do it for you (see pages 161–63).

> # Hot Tip
> Some web hosts do not let you import web files created elsewhere, so make sure whoever you choose to host your website accepts them.

SEARCH-ENGINE FRIENDLY

While we'll go into more detail about how to optimize your website for search engines a bit later in this book, you can take a few steps before you launch your website to ensure you have made it search-engine friendly.

Above: If your web editor has any SEO functionality, make sure you take advantage of it.

- **Page SEO:** Some website builders have an SEO function. This enables you to add metadata (information used by search engines) to each page, such as description, keywords, location and site name.

→ **Keywords:** Have you included words in your content that users will type into a search engine to find you? Keywords can make it easy for search engines to bring you up after search requests.

→ **Navigation:** Is every page on your website linked together in a simple, easy-to-navigate structure?

→ **Links:** Make sure you link to your website from your social media pages.

GOING LIVE

Before you go live, you will of course have to choose your hosting service. Many web hosts offer various packages, so you will have to choose whichever package suits your needs. Usually hosting is done on a yearly basis, and you may have to pay for it in advance before your site goes live.

Below: If you want to use your own web address, you may have to upgrade your hosting service.

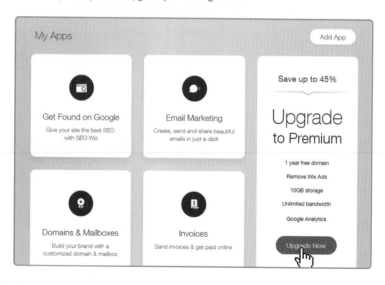

Hosting Requirements

You can get free web hosting if you do not mind using the domain name of your web host and do not require large amounts of bandwidth or storage. However if you want to use your own domain name, you need to work out how popular you think your website will be, and how large you think the website will grow in the next 12 months.

WEB DEVELOPMENT

Websites are never 'finished' and require regular maintenance and development. You may want to add more pages in the future if, for instance, you increase the range of products your business sells, or you may want to update the themes and colours. Fashions change and what may look like a well-designed, modern-looking website today may start to look a bit jaded in a few years' time.

Making Changes

You can usually edit your website at any time. If you created it on your web host, it may be a simple matter of logging in and clicking 'Edit'. This can make altering your website very easy. If you uploaded your files to your web host, you may have to replace the files by uploading the edited versions.

Below: If you have built your website online it shouldn't be difficult to edit it once it is live.

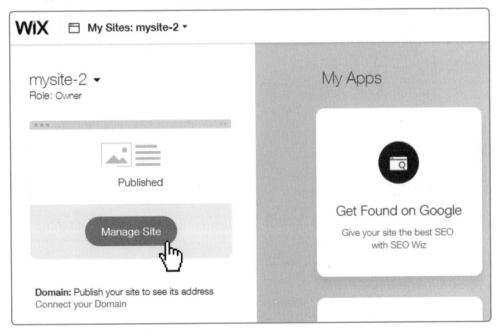

THINGS TO REMEMBER

If you are creating a basic website, the process can be quite straightforward but there are a few things to remember. If this is your first website, then you really should start small. Avoid trying to create complicated, large websites full of different types of content. Keep it simple – a homepage and one or two more pages. You can always add and restructure a website later, but it is better to walk before you can run.

Type of Website

You can create some good but simple business and even e-commerce websites on an online editor, but if you want a more sophisticated web presence, you may want to consider taking

Below: Keep your design simple to begin with. You can always improve it later on.

another approach. For personal websites, the basic approach is often the simplest and easiest method of getting online.

SOME DESIGN PRINCIPLES

- → **Consistency**: When it comes to good web design, consistency is key. Keep to a small palette of colours, fonts and styles.

- → **Layout**: Keep layouts simple. Be formulaic with your web pages. Keep your elements in the same location, so if you have an image in one place on one page, put an image in the same place on another page.

- → **Themes**: Make sure your website represents your business or how you want people to see you. Choose themes, colours and content carefully.

- → **Above the fold**: Remember people scroll down websites. Put all your important information at the top.

Right: A simple design has a better chance of looking good and working well on a mobile device.

Jargon Buster

All the content a person sees when they first click on a web page is 'above the fold'; things they have to scroll down to see are 'below the fold'.

INTERMEDIATE WEBSITE DESIGN

TAKING YOUR WEBSITE FURTHER

If you want to use your own domain name, or have an existing website to upgrade, or you want to build a website from scratch, an online web editor might not the best solution for you. However, thanks to the array of tools available, you can still achieve all of this.

WYSIWYG

Just because you are not using a web host's design platform, does not mean you cannot take advantage of a WYSIWYG design tool. Programs such as Dreamweaver or RapidWeaver let you do many of the same things that simpler tools allow, as well as providing many more functions. However, most importantly, they give you access to the website's code, so you can make manual changes and clean up the HTML.

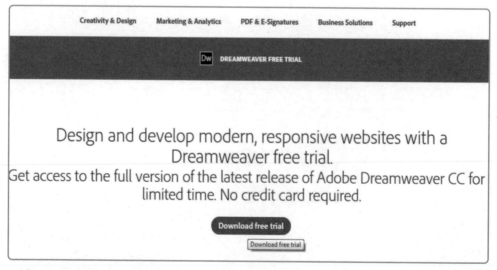

Above: Dreamweaver is available as part of Adobe Creative Cloud, or as a single program, but you can download a free trial.

SOFTWARE

While many web design programs claim to be a one-tool solution for web design, that is rarely the case. Software you may find useful includes:

→ **Web building**: Programs such as Dreamweaver, RapidWeaver, Adobe Muse, Macaw and Sketch allow you to design websites without knowing much code.

Hot Tip

Using a WYSIWYG HTML editor is a great way to learn and understand HTML, as you can see the code created before your eyes.

→ **Design**: You can manipulate images and create graphics on programs such as Photoshop, Gimp and Paint.NET, while a program such as Adobe Illustrator will let you create illustrations and graphics.

Hot Tip

Professional web design software can be costly, but many offer a time-limited free trial, and you can generally find comparable software that is open-source and free.

→ **Development**: Notepad++ and Sublime Text are text editors, useful for handling HTML.

→ **Planning**: Microsoft Word is a good tool for writing content, while Microsoft Excel can help you plan and create your structure and how the various pages link to one another.

Notes - Notepad

File Edit Format View Help

Above: A simple program such as MS Notepad is perfect for writing out HTML.

USING DREAMWEAVER

While some web design programs offer more functionality than others and some have a quicker learning curve, they can be very similar to use. Dreamweaver is among the most popular and, for that reason, it is a good platform for the intermediate web designer as there is no shortage of online assistance in forums and help pages to help you get to grips with the program.

Downloading Dreamweaver

Dreamweaver can be downloaded as a single program or part of Adobe Creative Cloud.

1.   Visit: http://www.adobe.com/uk/products/dreamweaver.html and click on 'Buy Now'.

2.   If you want to download just Dreamweaver, select it under 'Single App' and click 'Buy Now'. If you want to buy it with other programs, select the appropriate package.

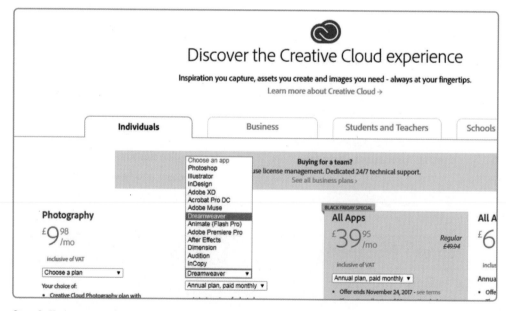

Step 2. Choose your package.

3.   The Dreamweaver install will download. Open the program, click 'Install' and follow the instructions (the program will automatically install on download for Mac users).

Organizing your Files

Dreamweaver organizes all the documents on your computer associated with your website. A Dreamweaver site usually has two parts:

↪ **Local folder**: The working directory, often a folder on your hard drive, where all your web files are kept.

↪ **Remote folder**: Where you store your files on your web server.

Hot Tip

Dreamweaver has a number of basic templates you can use and it can often be much easier to use one of these to start creating your bespoke website.

Documents library
businesssolutionwebtemplate

Name	Date modified	Type	Size
_notes	27/11/2017 16:49	File folder	
css	27/11/2017 17:16	File folder	
images	27/11/2017 17:28	File folder	
Dreamweaver CSS file	27/11/2017 16:18	Cascading Style S...	1 KB
about	04/04/2014 06:14	Firefox HTML Doc...	4 KB
blog	04/04/2014 06:14	Firefox HTML Doc...	5 KB
contact	04/04/2014 06:14	Firefox HTML Doc...	3 KB
index	27/11/2017 17:38	Firefox HTML Doc...	2 KB
news	04/04/2014 06:14	Firefox HTML Doc...	3 KB
product	04/04/2014 06:14	Firefox HTML Doc...	4 KB
services	04/04/2014 06:14	Firefox HTML Doc...	3 KB
solutions	04/04/2014 06:14	Firefox HTML Doc...	3 KB
businesssolutionwebtemplate.psd	04/04/2014 06:14	PSD File	23,882 KB

Type: Firefox HTML Document
Size: 2.87 KB
Date modified: 04/04/2014 06:14

Above: A local folder on a hard drive containing website files created by Dreamweaver.

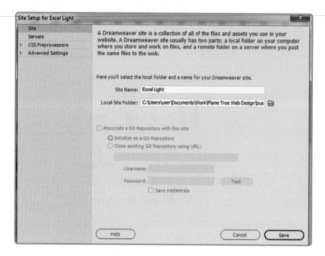

Step 3. Selecting the Local Site Folder.

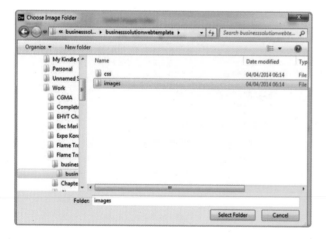

Step 5. Choosing your image folder.

GETTING STARTED

1. If you are using a template or working on an existing project, click 'File' and 'Open' and select the HTML (.htm) document. Otherwise, just click new and select 'New Document'.

2. To tell Dreamweaver you are working on a website and where the files are kept, select 'Site', click 'New Site...' and name your project.

3. Now select the folder containing your template files in 'Local Site Folder'.

4. Next expand the 'Advanced Settings' on the left of the Site Setup dialog box, and select 'Local Info'.

5. Define where your image folder is. This tells Dreamweaver to automatically copy images to this folder when you import them from outside the root folder.

6. There's no need to insert a value for Web URL unless you are working with a live website. So just click 'Save'.

DREAMWEAVER VIEWS

Like most web design software, Dreamweaver offers you the ability to see your website code as you create it. At the top you can choose one of three views:

- **Code**: The HTML for your web page.

- **Split**: Splits the screen between a WYSIWYG view and the code – the recommended option for creating a website.

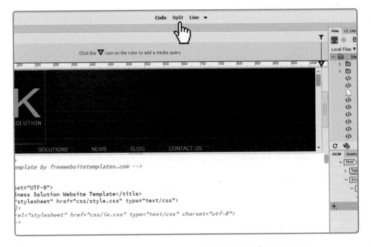

Above: You can have a split view of code and WYSIWYG on Dreamweaver.

- **Live**: Choose between 'Live', and see your website as it would appear on the Web or 'Design' and make changes easily.

DOM Panel

The Document Object Model (DOM) panel creates a tree structure of your page elements. This helps you map elements in Live View with the respective HTML code. You can also make edits to the HTML structure in the DOM panel and see changes instantly take effect in Live View.

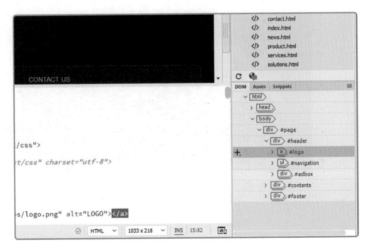

Above: The DOM panel.

Assets and Snippets

In the next tab of the DOM panel is 'Assets'. The Assets panel can help you keep track and preview assets stored on your site, such as images, movies and links.

The Snippets panel is used to speed up the process of writing code. By saving code as a snippet, you can double-click it in the Snippets panel to insert it in multiple places.

HTML and CSS

You can view both the HTML source code for your website and its CSS style sheet by using the tabs at the top left of the working panel, just beneath the menu buttons. This means things you can make changes to, such as colour, font and the position of elements, using the same CSS for all pages.

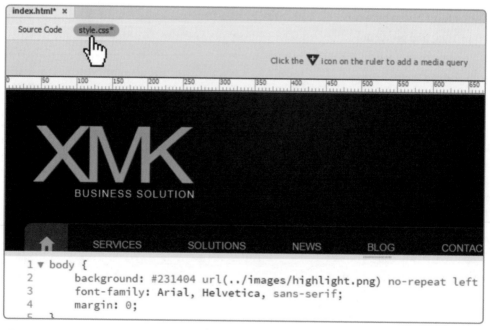

Above: You can choose to view source (HTML) or CSS code.

Files and Library

At the top right of the working panel above the Assets and Snippets window is where you can control and see all the web pages connected to your website, as well as add new elements and upload files to the Cloud.

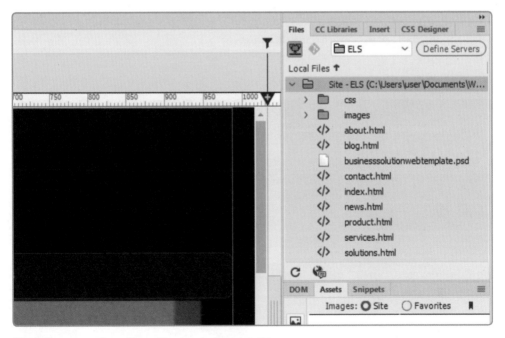

➔ **Files:** Here you can see all the files associated with your website, including HTML documents for separate web pages, your image folders and CSS documents.

➔ **CC Libraries:** A web service that allows you to upload, store and download assets across various Adobe desktop and mobile applications, including Dreamweaver and Photoshop.

➔ **Insert:** Here you can add elements to a web page, such as images, paragraphs, tables and links.

Above: You can see all your files and insert more elements in this menu.

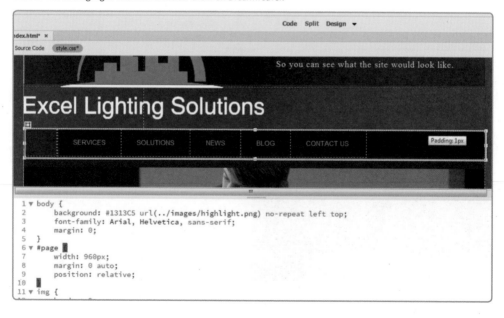 **CSS Designer**: This panel lets you visually create CSS styles, files, and set properties, along with media queries to control the screen size.

MAKING CHANGES

There are no hard and fast rules about how to make changes in programs such as Dreamweaver. In fact, you can do almost anything in a number of ways:

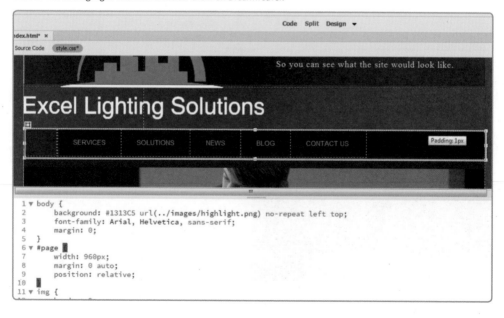 **Code**: You can directly alter the HTML or CSS code to change colours, styles and the position of elements.

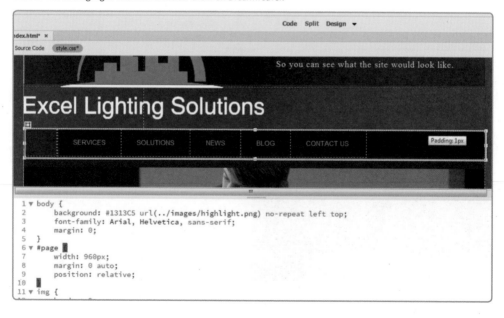 **Design**: The design mode lets you drag and drop items in the same way you can when using simple online website design tools.

Below: You can highlight elements and alter them on Dreamweaver.

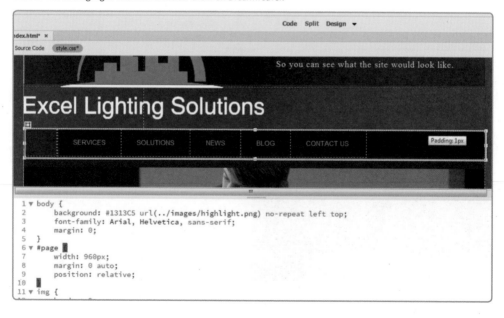

Quick Edit: A quick edit mode lets you right-click on an element in HTML or CSS, such as a colour code, and change it using a colour palette.

USING CSS

The great thing about programs such as Dreamweaver is that you can make changes to cascading style sheets, so any change you make on say the homepage, such as changes to the header, background and so on, you can replicate on all subsequent pages.

Creating a CSS Document

If you are using a template you have uploaded to Dreamweaver, you will already most likely have a CSS style sheet. If you do not, or you are building a site from scratch, you will want to create a CSS file.

1. Click File in the top menu and select 'New Document'.

2. Under 'Document Type', select CSS and click 'Create'.

3. Now click 'File' and 'Save as' and save the file to your website directory and give it a name such as 'dreamweaver-styles.css' (the .css is added automatically).

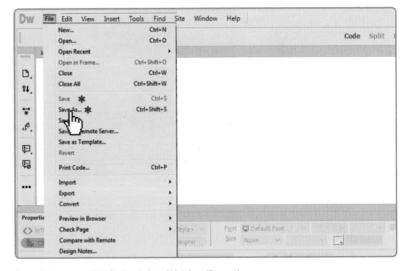

Step 3. Save your CSS file by clicking 'File' then 'Save as'.

Linking Your CSS File to Your Template

In order to assign a CSS styles to your template, you will need to link the two together:

1.   Click 'File' and select 'Attach Style Sheet'.

2.   Click 'Browse' and then the 'Site Root'.

Step 2. Attaching a style sheet.

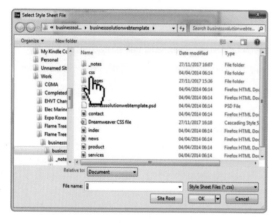

Step 3. Selecting your CSS file.

3.   Select your CSS file and click 'OK'. If this is an existing template, select the style sheet in your CSS folder.

4.   Finally, in the 'Attaching Existing CSS File' dialog box, click 'OK'.

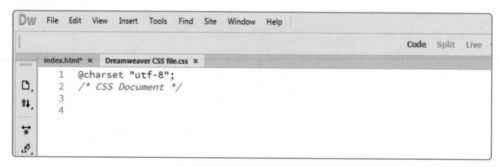

Above: A (nearly blank) CSS file attached to the website in Dreamweaver.

MAKE STYLE CHANGES

If you want to make style changes to your website so they translate to every page, you can edit your CSS file.

1. Make sure you are in 'Design' mode.

2. Right-click the element you want to change in the top pane and select 'Page Properties'.

3. Choose the aspect of the element you want to change, such as 'Background Colour' and click it.

4. Choose the new colour or style (you can add hex colour codes by pasting the number next to the colour box).

Alternatively, you can make the changes directly to the CSS file:

1. Find the element you want to change in the CSS file, such as a colour code.

2. Right-click the element, and select 'Quick Edit'.

3. Choose either a new colour from the colour palette or type in the colour code in the box.

4. Press enter.

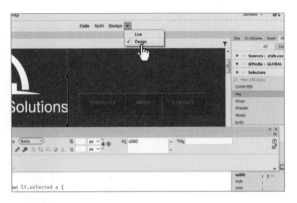

Step 1. Selecting 'Design' mode.

Step 2. Selecting page properties.

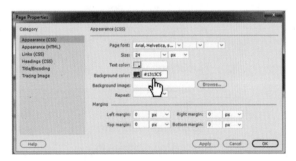

Step 4. Choosing your colour or style.

USING BLUEGRIFFON

While Dreamweaver is much favoured by professional web designers, for those embarking on their first website or wanting to get into web design, BlueGriffon provides much of the same functionality as Dreamweaver but it can be a little easier to use, and it is also available to download for free.

Download BlueGriffon

1. Visit: http://bluegriffon. org and click the 'Download' tab.

2. Choose the Windows, Mac or Linux version you want to download.

3. BlueGriffon will be downloaded as a zip file. Extract and run the program (click the application program in the BlueGriffon folder).

Step 2. Choosing a version of BlueGriffon to download.

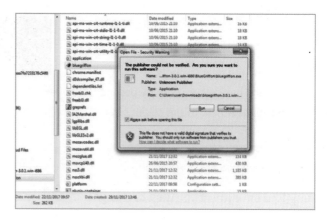

Step 3. Double-clicking the application file will install BlueGriffon.

Hot Tip

To make things easier, BlueGriffon has a web-building wizard, which guides you through the entire web-building process.

CREATING A NEW WEB PAGE

To create a web page using BlueGriffon:

1. Click 'File' then select 'New wizard' from the menu.

2. Select the Document Type. By default, 'HTML5' should be selected. If not, select it and click 'Next'.

3. Enter the document meta properties, including Title, Author (optional), Description and Keywords.

4. Now select the colour properties for your web page and click 'Next'.

5. Choose a background image if required.

6. Leave the 'Apply a predefined CSS layout' box unchecked and click 'Finish'.

7. Before you edit your website, make sure you save it to a root file by clicking 'Save As' and then choose a location.

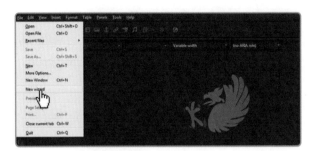

Step 1. Selecting 'New wizard'.

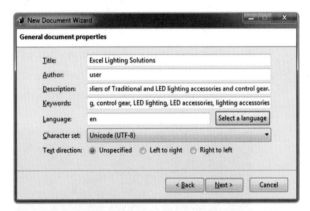

Step 3. Entering meta properties.

Step 5. Installing a background image.

Views

As with Dreamweaver, you can select WYSIWYG, source (code) and print preview views, or you can opt for a split view (WYSIWYG and code).

ADJUSTING YOUR WEB PAGE

The initial web page will contain placeholder text. At the top are the words 'PAGE HEADER'. These words reside in a horizontal band that stretches across the width of your web page. You can replace this text with your company name or company logo. To add a logo:

1.   Click your mouse where it says 'PAGE HEADER'.

2.   Click 'Insert' then select 'Image' from the main menu.

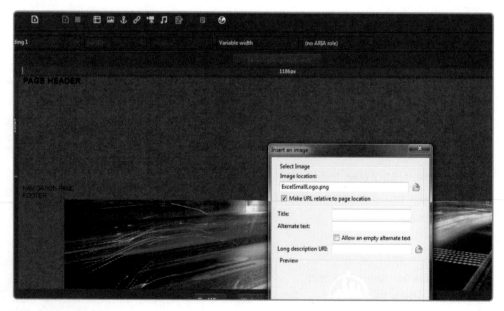

Step 2. Selecting a logo.

3.   Select your image. Check the 'Make URL relative to page location'. You can 'Allow an empty alternate text' by checking that box.

4.   Click 'OK' and your picture should now appear in the header section of your web page.

Making Changes

You can make changes in BlueGriffon in a number of ways:

→ **Style properties**: If you select 'Panels' from the main menu and choose 'Style Properties' you can make all sorts of adjustments to text size, colours, position, layout and borders.

→ **Quick menu:** The left-hand menu lets you make quick changes such as justification, text colour and bold/ italic styles.

→ **HTML**: As with Dreamweaver, you can delve into the HTML and make changes directly to the code.

Above: You can change fonts easily in the drop-down menu.

USING HTML

If you are using tools such as Dreamweaver or BlueGriffon, then a basic knowledge of HTML is going to help a lot.

WYSIWYG AND HTML

When creating a website on an online design platform, it can be easy to forget that the creation before your eyes is a façade, and what you are really doing is creating a load of HTML code to tell a web browser what to display. All this is done behind the scenes, but you can view the code by choosing a split screen in your web design software and make changes directly into the code. This can help create cleaner websites and more specific functionality than just relying on the WYSIWYG tools.

```
                    SERVICES         SOLUTIONS         NEWS          BLOG          CON
1 ▼ body {
2          background: #231404 url(../images/highlight.png) no-repeat l
3          font-family: Arial, Helvetica, sans-serif;
4          margin: 0;
5   }
6 ▼ #page {
7          width: 960px;
8          margin: 0 auto;
9          position: relative;
0   }
1 ▼ img {
2          border: 0;
3   }
4    /*--------------------------------- SPRITES ---------------------
5 ▼ #navigation li:first-child a, #main ul li, #main ul li a, #headl
6          background: url(../images/buttons.png) no-repeat;
```

Above: Everything you do with a WYSIWYG tool gets translated into HTML.

HTML TAGS

All HTML documents are collections of tags, enclosed within less than (<) and greater than (>) signs. Most are also container tags, that is they have an opening tag (such as <i>) and a closing tag (</i>). The tags tell the browser how to display anything that is contained within the tags. So, <i> this text is shown in italics </i>.

Modifying Tags

Tags can be modified by attributes, stated in the opening tag, which allow you to specify properties such as font, size, colour, and so on. For example, <font colour="#FF0000"> puts the text in red. In HTML, if an attribute has a value, that is a single word or number, it does not need to go between quote marks. Similarly, HTML itself is not case-sensitive, so <FONT> is the same as <font>.

```
19  p{font-size: 18px;}
20  .bg{background: #eee; padding:40px; display: inline-block;}
21  </style>
22
23  </head>
24  <body>
25  <div id="container">
26  <div class="bg">
27  <img src="images/SmallLogo.png" alt="This website is currently under constructio
28  <hr>
29  <h1>Our Site is Currently Under Construction</h1>
30  <p>For more information contact Us with the following details</p>
31  <h2>Excel Lighting Solutions<br>
32  396 Tonbridge Road<br>
33  Maidstone<br>
34  Kent<br>
35  ME16 9LW</h2>
36
37  <h2><a href="tel:01622 205540">01622 205540</a></h2>
38  <h2><a href="mailto:Sales@excellightingsolutions.co.uk"> Sales@excellightingsolu
39  </div>
40  </body>
41  </html>
```

Above: Tags are opened with <> and closed with </>.

HTML DOCUMENT PARTS

Each HTML document has two main parts, the <head>, which contains general information about the file and the scripts that need to be run, and the <body>, which is the content that will appear in the browser window. Normally, this HTML outline for the page will be automatically set up by your web-authoring program.

Hot Tip

Use headers for greater visual emphasis. There are six available, <h1> being the biggest and <h6> the smallest (too small for most viewers). With most browsers, <h4> is equivalent to the size of the body text.

Document Type

Typically, the page will start with a document type definition, which lets the browser know which HTML standard you are following. Within the head, you should also include the <title>, which has the text that will appear in the browser's title bar (for example, <title>My Web Page</title>).

```
1  <!DOCTYPE HTML PUBLIC "-//W3C//DTD HTML 4.01 Transitional//EN" "ht
2  <html>
3  <head>
4  <title>This website is currently under construction</title>
5
6  <meta http-equiv="content-type" content="text/html; charset=iso-88
7  <meta name="keywords" content="This website is currently under con
8  <meta name="description" content="This website is currently under
9  <meta name="author" content="www.SiteWizard.co.uk">
10
11 <style type="text/css" media="screen">
12
13 html { border-top:5px solid #752a90;  }
14 body { margin:0 padding:0; text-align:center; font:70% tahoma, san
15 #container { margin:120px auto 0 auto; width:100%; max-width:600px
16 h1{color:#262161;}
17 h2{color:#262161;}
18 a{color:#262161;}
```

Above: A web page has a <head>, a <body> and a <title>.

Body

The <body> tag surrounds the entire visible content of a page, and its attributes define the colour of the document and its text content. However, in many instances, CSS now make it unnecessary to include attributes in HTML.

Paragraphs and Breaks

Standard HTML has two ways of breaking lines. The paragraph tag <p> inserts a double-line break at the end of each paragraph, while the line-break tag <br> merely breaks a line at the point where the tag is added. <p> can carry the 'class' attribute, which defines a style for the whole paragraph according to an attached style sheet. Paragraphs should be closed using </p>. Extra emphasis can be given to a line break by adding a horizontal rule using the <hr> tag. Variables include 'width' (in pixels or per cent) and 'color'.

```
19  p{font-size: 18px;}
20  .bg{background: #eee; padding:40px; display: inline-block;}
21  </style>
22
23  </head>
24  <body>
25  <div id="container">
26  <div class="bg">
27  <img src="images/SmallLogo.png" alt="This website is currently und
28  <hr>
29  <h1>Our Site is Currently Under Construction</h1>
30  <p>For more information contact Us with the following details</p>
31  <h2>Excel Lighting Solutions<br>
32  396 Tonbridge Road<br>
33  Maidstone<br>
34  Kent<br>
35  ME16 9LW</h2>
36
37  <h2><a href="tel:01622 205540">01622 205540</a></h2>
```

Above: Paragraph tags <p> </p> and line breaks
 </br> are used to format text.

Anchor or Hyperlink Tags

The 'href' attribute specifies the destination page, while the `<target>` tag places the linked page into a frame or a new window. You can use the 'name' attribute elsewhere on a page to place an anchor. All the elements between the `<a>` and `</a>` tags will become an active hyperlink.

Style Tags

Inline styles are put in the flow of the text to add emphasis, without affecting spacing in the way block element tags such as paragraph breaks do. Inline styles can italicize text `<i>...</i>`; embolden it `<b>...</b>`; or add an underline `<u>...</u>`. You can change the default font size by using the `<basefont>` tag; however, the `<font>` tag is unnecessary if you are using CSS.

```
!DOCTYPE html>
html>
    <head>
        <title>The bold, italic and underline tags</titl
    </head>
    <body>
        <p><b>This will be in bold</b></p>
        <p><i>This will be in italic</i></p>
        <p><u>This will be underlined</u></p>
    </body>
/html>
```

Above: HTML allows you to adjust text styles of specific text, although CSS can be used to create styles for all text on pages.

IMAGE TAGS

The <img> tag places an inline image into a page. The location of the image is specified by the 'src' attribute. The 'align' attribute specifies the position of the image in relation to the page ('left', 'right', 'center') or in relation to the line of text ('top', 'middle', 'bottom').

```
<BODY>

          <IMG SRC="home.jpg">
          <P>
          <IMG SRC="home2.jpg">

          <P>
          <INPUT TYPE="button" value=" GO " on

          <P>
          <LABEL ID="label_1">Image Names</LAB

          <SCRIPT LANGUAGE = "Javascript">

          </SCRIPT>
</BODY>
```

Above: Image tags will place an image into a web page, in this case the images home.jpg and home2.jpg.

Spacing

The 'vspace' and 'hspace' attributes define the amount of pixels placed around the image, while 'alt' defines text that appears until the image loads completely. 'Height' and 'width' can also be specified, usually to create a placeholder rather than to resize the image, unless a single-pixel spacer is used.

Tables

The `<table>` tag defines the position of a table and, like an image, uses the 'align' attribute. Its 'border' attribute sets the thickness of the bevelled border, and 'bgcolor' and 'background' properties work as they do for the `<body>` tag (we will look at tables in more detail on pages 212–214).

META TAGS

These document information tags are a way of including information about a document and the content it contains. Meta data is used by search engines to describe and categorize web pages. Meta tags, which must be nested inside the head of a web page, hold hidden information about the document. Invisible to the reader, this is picked up by servers, browsers or search engines and acted on. Meta tags include:

```
name="viewport" content="width=device-width,initial-scale=1,maximum-scale=1.0,user-
scalable=0"><meta
name="msapplication-TileColor" content="#da532c"><meta
name="msapplication-TileImage" content="/mstile-144x144.png"><meta
name="theme-color" content="#ffffff"><meta
name="keywords" content="Buy lights, Lighting Company,wall lights, large
lighting,lighting companies, light company,lights for barns, high ceilings lights,
lights for low ceilings, lighting suppliers, Ceiling Lights, hanging light, hanging
lighting, pendants Lights, lanterns, wall lighting, indoor lights, external lighting.
Lighting for homes and business,Home lighting, buy lighting online. Modern lights,
contemporary lights, retro lights, lanterns, pendant, kitchen island lights, lighting
UK" /><meta
name="description" content="Lighting specialists - buy thousands of lights online.
Lighting for every room inside your home and outdoors too. Spend £50 for Free UK
```

Above: Meta tags such as keywords are used by search engines.

Name: Normally contains information about the content of the page, such as the author's name and details of the copyright, as well as two tags.

Description: Describes the content of your web page. The description will appear on the search results page.

Keywords: Used by many search engines for categorizing and indexing documents.

STYLE SHEETS

HTML's table tags and cascading style sheets (CSS) have added tools for creating grids that can align objects and include the designer's best friend – white space. The arrival of style sheets has meant that designers also have much fuller control over the look and feel of a page. Style sheets provide a centrally stored set of definitions for different layout attributes, such as text size, line spacing or indents. A single definition can be applied site-wide, so changes can be done in one hit rather than being applied to each specific instance. Read more about style sheets in 'Advanced Web Design' on pages 174–81.

```
<table style="width:100%">
  <tr>
    <td>Jill</td>
    <td>Smith</td>
    <td>50</td>
  </tr>
  <tr>
    <td>Eve</td>
    <td>Jackson</td>
    <td>94</td>
  </tr>
</table>
```

Above: The HTML tables allow web authors to arrange data like text, images, links, other tables into rows and columns of cells.

IMAGE SOFTWARE

If you are using images on your website then image software can help you edit your images. However, that's not all; you can use image software to design your entire website.

PHOTOSHOP

By far the most commonly used image software is Adobe Photoshop. Originally designed as a graphic design package, Photoshop, and similar programs to it, let you manipulate and adjust images in an almost unlimited number of ways:

Below: Photoshop is widely used by web designers for creating graphics and editing images.

➔ **Layers**: Programs such as Photoshop let you create layers. This enables you to place images on top of one another – great for creating logos, headers and banners.

➔ **Retouching**: You can change the colours, use the clone tool to hide or remove aspects of an image, and airbrush pictures to get them to look just how you want.

➔ **Cropping/Resizing**: Reducing image sizes can help images load faster, and you can also crop images to ensure you are using only the parts of an image you want.

> ## Hot Tip
>
> Be careful when resizing images. The smaller an image, the fewer the pixels and the quicker it will download but the less detail will be shown in the picture. Try to get the balance right.

➔ **Reformatting**: You can change the image formats to make them more web-friendly.

LAYERS

Layers are a great way of creating graphic files. For instance, if you want to place a logo on top of a background image, you can do this by creating two layers, one for the background and one for the logo.

Using Layers

1. Open the image software and create a new file. Add your background image by using 'File' and 'Open', or by dragging your image file into position.

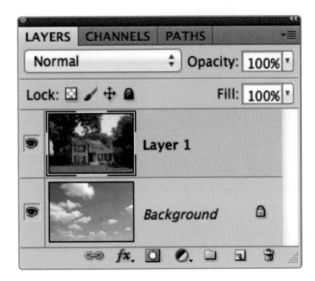

Above: Layers let you place images over images.

Step 2. Adding a new layer in Paint.Net.

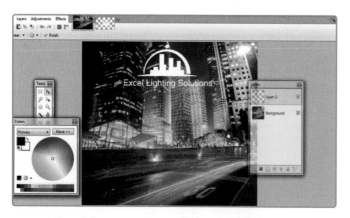

Step 4. You can superimpose images on top of one another.

2. Select 'Layers' from the main menu or hold down CTRL, Shift and N (to create a new layer).

3. Add your next image to the new layer by opening it or dragging it into position.

4. You can move the image anywhere you want and the background image will be untouched by the addition of the new image over the top of it.

Flattening Images

You cannot use a layered image on your website. Instead you have to flatten it (merge the layers together). You can do this either by selecting 'Merge Layer Down' from the main menu, or agreeing to flatten the image when you save it as a JPEG or other web-friendly format.

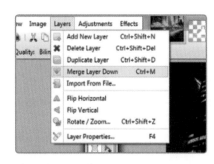

PHOTOSHOP AS A DESIGN TOOL

Increasingly, web designers are using Photoshop or other image software to create entire web pages.

Above: You have to flatten images by merging them to remove layers before you can use them on the Web.

1. Create a new document. Enter your chosen dimensions – 800px x 1200px is quite standard for creating a new website.

2. Use a background image or plain background (you can fill a white background in any colour by using the bucket tool).

Step 2. Using a background image.

3. Create a new layer for your header. Add your text or logo to the header.

4. Create navigation buttons in a new layer. Use the rectangular, bucket and text tools to create each button.

5. Add your content, footers, banners and other web elements.

Step 4. Creating navigation buttons.

Slicing

It is advisable to leave the content area of your website blank, as using Photoshop or other image software means you are saving your website as image slices. To do this, use the slice tool to give names to all your web elements. Mark the area that is the header with the slice tool and name it 'header', mark the area of the home button and name it 'home button', and so on.

Export the slices to a new file. This will create an HTML file, a CSS file and an images folder with all the different slices and images inside it. Use the same HTML page for each web page (copy and paste), and add text and other content to your files using OneNote or Notepad.

Left: Photoshop's slice tool can separate all your elements so you can name them and use them individually.

BACKGROUND IMAGES

Using a background image can add a lot of interest to a page. A background graphic can fill the browser screen without taking up all the bandwidth, although it will load more slowly than a page with a solid background colour. Bear in mind that the image does not need to be the size of the space it will eventually fill, as the browser will expand it to fill the page.

Choosing a Background Image

Images can be any web graphic as long as it is correctly formatted – whether a picture, a textured pattern or a piece of clip art. However, while textured backgrounds are good because they add a bit of depth to your web page, remember that they can make the text very difficult to read if they are too obtrusive.

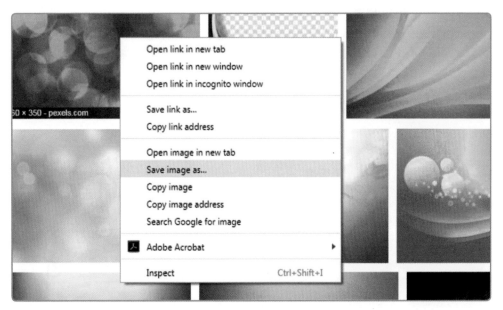

Above: There are plenty of image resources on the Web such as www.1001freedownloads.com/free-cliparts/.

SOURCING IMAGES

There are plenty of ways to acquire images. There is an abundance of graphics available on the Web, and digital cameras and smartphones make it easy to capture the picture you want.

- **Scanning**: If you have an image you want to use on paper you can scan it, but you must keep the resolution to a manageable size.

- **Web images**: You can download or copy images from the Web. The great thing about these images is that they are already tailored for use on web pages.

- **Clip art**: The Web is full of places where you can buy (or download for free) clip art and images.

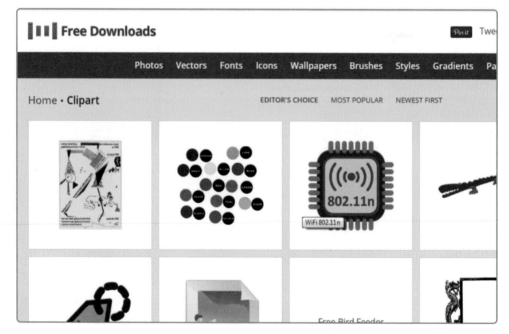

Above: You can save images from the Web very easily by right-clicking and selecting 'Save image as...'.

GOING LIVE

Once you have created your website offline, you will need to upload it to your web host, and that may require additional software.

FTP HOST

In order to upload your website to your host server, you will need certain information:

- **FTP server**: The name of the FTP server for your website. This may look something like 'ftp.mywebhost.com'.

- **User ID**: Your web host will provide you with a user ID and password to log in to your FTP account.

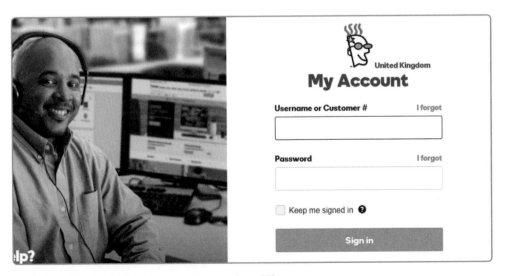

Above: You will need login details for your web host and your FTP account.

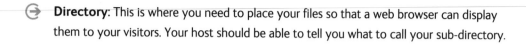 **Directory**: This is where you need to place your files so that a web browser can display them to your visitors. Your host should be able to tell you what to call your sub-directory.

No FTP

Not all web hosts require FTP uploads and you can use whatever method they have designated for you to upload your files.

UPLOADING FILES

To upload your website from your computer to your web host, you may need an FTP client. Programs such as Dreamweaver have their own FTP client built in, but the tool most people turn to for FTP transfers is Filezilla.

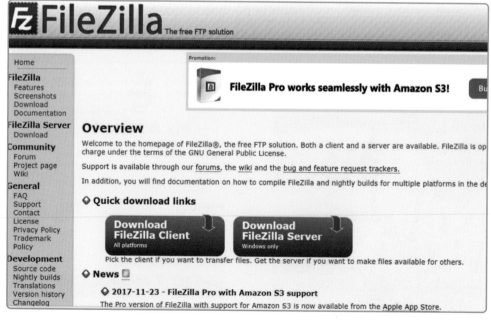

Above: Filezilla is a popular FTP client.

Filezilla

Filezilla is an open-source FTP solution that works for both client and host. It is free to download from https://filezilla-project.org/ and is available for Windows, Linux and macOS. FileZilla allows you to upload all sorts of files, from HTML documents to images, video clips, music files (for example, MP3 files, WAV files, MIDI files) and entire directories (folders) containing all your files.

UPLOADING TO YOUR WEB SERVER

To begin the process of transferring your website to your web host using Filezilla:

1.   Click 'New Site' and give it the name of your website.

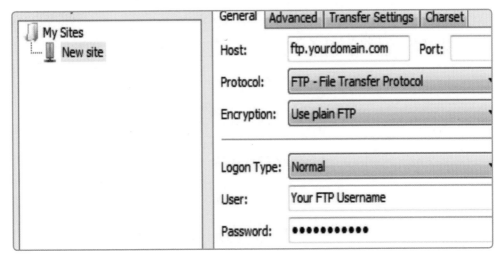

Step 2. Enter the name of your FTP server in 'Host'.

2.   Under the 'General' tab, enter the name of your FTP server in the 'Host' input box. For example, if your web host told you that the FTP host name is 'ftp.webhost.com', enter this into the space provided.

3. Select 'Normal' for 'Logon Type', and enter the user ID and password for your web host.

4. Click 'Connect'. FileZilla should log in to your server.

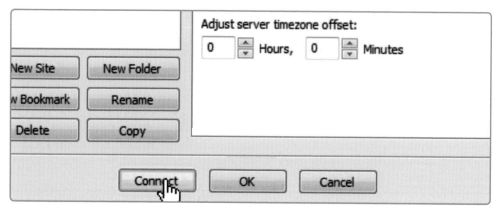

Step 4. Click 'Connect'.

5. Locate the website files you want to upload in the 'Local Site' window. Drag the files to the 'Remote Site' Window (or you can right-click the file and select 'Upload').

6. Your files should now be transferred. When complete, disconnect from your website by clicking the 'Server' menu followed by 'Disconnect'.

TESTING

When you have uploaded your website you need to test everything fully. This is not just a case of ensuring all the links work and that your web pages look the way you intended in your browser, but you also need to test for other browsers and other devices.

Browsers: Download various different browsers and ensure your website looks and runs well in them all. Different browsers can react differently to HTML, especially discrepancies or minor errors in the code, so if something doesn't look right, it could be an indication of an error.

→ **Mobiles/Tablets**: Your website should look good and navigate well even on the smallest of screens. If you find issues in the way mobile devices display your website, you may have to design a mobile-friendly version to accompany your original site.

ADDING TO YOUR WEBSITE

You should never regard your website as being finished. Think of it as a work in progress. You may come up with new ideas for the type of content you want to display, or you may want to update the website to keep up with trends. Ensure you keep copies of your web files and folders, so if you need to make any changes, you can do so, and then upload to your web host when you have finished.

Backing Up

As with any project you do on a computer, it is always a good idea to back up your website files. Use services like Dropbox or Google Docs to upload copies of your files to the Web.

Left: Dropbox is a great tool for backing up to the Cloud.

ADVANCED WEBSITE DESIGN

START MASTERING WEB DESIGN

For those who understand code, creating a website from scratch using HTML, CSS and other web languages is perhaps the surest method of getting the results you want.

WHY CODE?

For some web designers, coding website from scratch is the only way to go. Purists will argue that using design tools such as Dreamweaver is cheating and these programs create cluttered web pages, filled with unnecessary code, and are limited in functionality. Web coding, on the other hand, allows you complete freedom to design and create whatever you want.

Plan

As with any web-design method, you still need a good idea of what you want to create, so before you begin coding your website, sketch out how you want the website to look, what elements you will need and how many web pages the site will have.

```
1   <!DOCTYPE html PUBLIC "-//W3C//DTD XHTML 1.0 Transitional//EN"
2   "http://www.w3.org/TR/xhtml1/DTD/xhtml1-transitional.dtd">
3   <html xmlns="http://www.w3.org/1999/xhtml" lang="en" xml:lang="en">
4   <head>
5           <title>Glasurit</title>
6           <meta http-equiv="Content-Type" content="text/html; charset=utf-8" />
7           <meta name="ROBOTS" content="ALL" />
8           <meta name="MSSmartTagsPreventParsing" content="true" />
9           <meta name="description" content="Website of Glasurit from BASF" />
10
11          <!-- CSS -->
12          <link rel="pingback" href="http://www.glasurit.dreamhosters.com/xmlrpc.php" />
13          <link rel="stylesheet" href="http://www.glasurit.dreamhosters.com/wp-content/themes/g
14          <link href="http://www.glasurit.dreamhosters.com/wp-content/themes/glasurite-theme/cs
15          <!-- rollover script -->
16          <script src="http://www.glasurit.dreamhosters.com/wp-content/themes/glasurite-theme/s
17          <script type="text/javascript" src="http://www.glasurit.dreamhosters.com/wp-content/t
18          <script type="text/javascript" src="http://www.glasurit.dreamhosters.com/wp-content/t
19          <script type="text/javascript">
20              $(document).ready(function() {
```

Above: Coding a website may seem complicated at first, but web languages are not that hard to learn.

TOOLS

In theory, if you are creating a static HTML website, you do not really need any specialist software, just a text editor such as Notepad (Windows) or TextEdit (Mac). However, in reality, you may want to use graphics packages such as Photoshop and you may well want to use an HTML editor.

HTML Editor

HTML editors are not like WYSIWYG tools (although some do have preview modes); you cannot drag and drop elements and have the editor create the code for you. An HTML editor is just a text program that can help keep your code clean and organized, and detects when you open a tag and automatically closes it (to prevent errors and bugs).

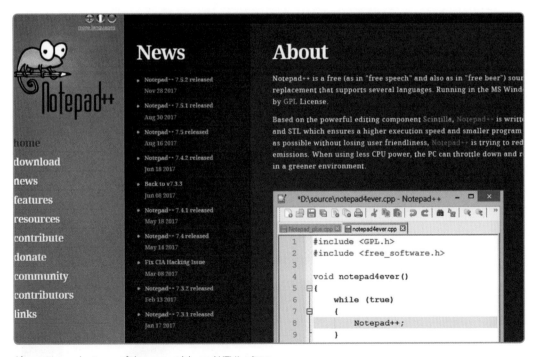

Above: Notepad++ is one of the most widely used HTML editors.

Some recommended HTML editors:

- **Notepad++**: https://notepad-plus-plus.org/. A free source code editor that supports several programming languages running under the MS Windows environment.

- **HTML-Kit**: www.htmlkit.com. A free HTML editor for Windows.

- **CoffeeCup**: www.coffeecup.com/html-editor. Both an HTML and CSS editor.

- **BBedit**: www.barebones.com/products/bbedit. HTML and text editor for the Mac.

FOUNDATIONS OF A WEB PAGE

While coding is part art, part science, the basic framework of a website is very simple. In fact, it takes just seconds to code a *very* basic website. For instance, the following will create a simple web page if you type it into your text editor and save as an HTML document:

```
<html>
<head>My Website<title>
</title>
</head>
<body>
<p>
This is the text to my website.
</p>
</body>
</html>
```

Above: A simple website created with a basic <head> and <body>.

ELEMENTS AND ATTRIBUTES

Of course, nobody wants a plain white web page with just a few words on it, so in order to build on the foundations of your website you will need to add elements and attributes.

Elements

In HTML, an element is anything written between (and including) tags. Therefore, when you open a tag, introduce content and then close it again, you have created an element. An element can be very basic, such as This is my element, or it can be much more complicated. In fact, you will often have elements within elements. This is because a website contains elements such as <body>, which encompasses all your content, so everything within the <body> tags is part of an element.

```
</title>
</head>
<body>
<p>
This is the text to my websit
</p>
</body>
</html>
```

Above: Elements are contained by tags.

Attributes

Sometimes when creating an element, we may want to add additional details, in which case we can use an attribute. Attributes define the characteristics of an element, such as alignment, font, size and so on. Attributes are made up of a name and a value.

For example:

```
<p align="center">My text element</p>
```

Above: You can centre text using the 'center' attribute.

In this example, the attribute is used to make the text element centred. The value of an attribute, in this case 'center', is placed inside quotation marks.

Hot Tip

HTML is written in American English, not British English, so spellings such as 'color' and 'center' are used.

META ELEMENTS

All web pages need a head element. Often this is the first thing a web designer will code
(although you do not have to). A head element contains a web page's meta data and is placed
between the <html> tag and the <body> tag. Head elements contain the <meta> element,
which is used to specify information for search engines, including the website's description,
keywords, author information and so on. The <meta> element also specifies the character set
that the HTML document uses.

Character Set

For HTML5, the default character encoding is UTF-8. For older versions of HTML, the character
encoding was ASCII. Put simply, the character set contains the letters (upper and lower case),
numbers, punctuation and some special characters that web pages can display. UTF-8 contains
far more characters than ASCII.

```
1  <!DOCTYPE html>
2  <html lang="en" class="home midcol">
3  <head>
4  <meta charset="utf-8" />
5  <title>Notepad++ Home</title>
6  <meta name="description" content="Notepad++: a free source code editor which supports several programming l
7  <meta name="keywords" content="Notepad++, telechargement, gratuit, free source code editor, remplacant de N
   editor, php editor, asp editor, javascript editor, java editor, c++ editor, c# editor, objective-c editor,
   Expression Search"/>
8
9  <link rel="alternate" type="application/rss+xml" title="Follow Notepad++ with RSS" href="/feed.rss"/>
10 <link rel="stylesheet" type="text/css" href="/assets/css/npp_c1.css"/>
11 <link rel="stylesheet" type="text/css" href="/assets/css/fonts/droidserif.css"/>
12 <link rel="shortcut icon" href="/assets/images/favicon.ico" type="image/x-icon" />
13 <!--[if lte IE 7]><link rel="stylesheet" type="text/css" href="/assets/css/ie67.css"/><![endif]-->
14
15
16
17 <script type="text/javascript">
18 window.__gcfg = {lang: 'en'};
19 (function()
20 {var po = document.createElement("script");
21 po.type = "text/javascript"; po.async = true;po.src = "https://apis.google.com/js/plusone.js";
22 var s = document.getElementsByTagName("script")[0];
23 s.parentNode.insertBefore(po, s);
24 })();</script>
25
26 <script type="text/javascript" src="https://code.jquery.com/jquery-1.5.min.js"></script>
27 <script type="text/javascript" src="/assets/js/npp_c1.js"></script>
28 <script type="text/javascript" src="https://apis.google.com/js/plusone.js"></script>
```

Above: <head> elements contain all the meta data.

CSS

HTML is not the only coding language you will need to create a website. CSS (Cascading Style Sheets) give website developers more control over the appearance of web pages than HTML.

THE JOY OF CSS

Cascading Style Sheets give web designers complete control over the layout and style of every element on a web page, from text and paragraphs to tables and page margins.

As the colour and layout attributes of entire sites can be set from a single remote CSS file, designers can make radical changes to the design of whole sites without having to edit hundreds

```
1   a,
2   button,
3   input[type="submit"] {
4       opacity: 1;
5       -webkit-transition: opacity .2s linear;
6       -moz-transition: opacity .2s linear;
7       -ms-transition: opacity .2s linear;
8       transition: opacity .2s linear;
9   }
10
11  h1, h2, h3, h4, h5, h6 {
12      font-weight: bold;
13      color: #333;
14  }
```

Above: Cascading Style Sheets let you set the layout for a website.

or thousands of individual HTML pages. Simply specifying a style name for each paragraph also reduces the size of HTML files considerably and speeds up page download times.

WEB PAGE FORMATTING

While you can format a web page using HTML, it can be a long and arduous process to ensure the styles, fonts and colours are the same across all your web pages. In fact, HTML was never designed for formatting at all.

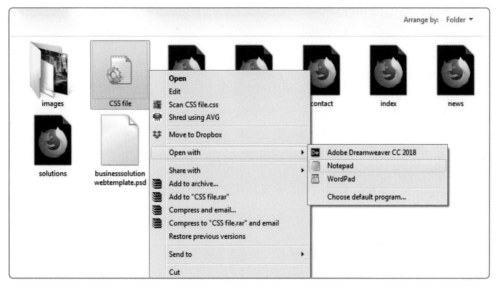

Above: CSS files can be edited and written in text editors much like HTML but they let you define attributes across an entire site.

Uses of CSS

Being able to define characters through a style sheet is much easier than having to refer to fonts and colour codes on every line, where the slightest error could put a page out of kilter with the rest of the site. If you just want to make a single change (to the size or colour of a site's main body font, for example), all you have to do is change the content of the CSS file.

FORMATTING WITH CSS

CSS removes the need to use formatting tags in HTML such as <font> or 'color' attributes.

Basic CSS consists of two aspects:

⊜ **Selector**: Points to the HTML element you want to style.

⊜ **Declaration**: Includes the style property and its value.

For example:

```
p {
        color: blue;
}
```

In this example, the selector is a paragraph, the declaration property is 'color' and the value is blue.

CSS Selectors

CSS goes even further than just enabling you to change specific HTML elements. You can also style unique elements, such as a particular paragraph, by inserting a hash (#) before the unique element (for example,

Hot Tip

The latest reiteration of CSS is CSS3. This latest standard is completely compatible with earlier version of CSS but has more functionality, including allowing you to round box corners, add borders to images and apply gradients and shadows to elements.

Below: CSS has a selector, in this case 'body', and a declaration (coloured red in this example) and a value (coloured blue).

```
<!DOCTYPE html>
<html>
<head>
<style>
body {
    background-color: red
    ;
}

h1 {
    color: white;
    text-align: center;
}

p {
```

#para1), or style all elements of a particular class, such as all centered items, by adding a full-stop (period) before a class of elements (for example, .center).

INSERTING CSS

You can insert a CSS in one of three ways:

- **Inline**: Used to apply a unique style for a single element.
- **External**: For changing the style of an entire website.
- **Internal**: For applying a unique style to a single web page.

Below: Using the # symbol you can apply CSS to unique elements.

```
<!DOCTYPE html>
<html>
<head>
<style>
#para1 {
    text-align: center;
    color: red;
}
</style>
</head>
<body>

<p id="para1">This text is a unique element with
CSS applied to it</p>
<p>This text has no CSS applied to it.</p>
```

This text is a unique element with CSS applied to it

This text has no CSS applied to it.

Inline Style Sheet

Applying an inline style sheet, you have to add the style attribute to the HTML document next to the specific element to which you want to apply it.

For example:

```
<h1 style="color:red;margin-right:20px;">My Top Heading</h1>
```

In the above example, the element, in this case the h1 header, will be 20px (pixels) from the right margin and will be coloured red.

External Style Sheet

External style sheets are slightly different as they have to be written separately, outside the HTML document in their own file. They can be written in a text editor like HTML documents but must not contain any html tags. External style sheets are saved using the .css extension.

For example:

```
body {
        background-color:  red;
}

h1  {
        color:  blue;
        margin-right:  20px;
```

In this example, every web page on a website will have a red background plus a blue header 20 pixels from the right margin.

Below: Inline style example.

```
<h1 style="color:red;margin-right:20px;">My Top Heading</h1>
```

Internal Style Sheet

Internal style sheets are written inside an HTML document and are defined using the `<style>` tag (inside the `<head>` section). The following example will give the same results as an external style sheet, but will apply to just one web page:

```
<head>
<style>
body {
    background-color: red;
}

h1 {
    color: blue;
    margin-right: 20px;
}
</style>
</head>
```

```
<head>
<style>
body {
    background-color: red;
}

h1 {
    color: blue;
    margin-right: 20px;
}
</style>
</head>
```

Above: Inline styles are inserted into HTML documents using the <style> tag.

CREATING AND APPLYING STYLE SHEETS

In CSS, elements such as type size and margin dimensions can be specified in pixels, points and millimetres rather than in the clumsy relative sizes used in HTML. Each page must include a reference to the external style sheet file, using the `<link>` element, which goes inside the HTML `<head>` section.

For example:

```
<head>
<link rel="stylesheet" type="text/css" href="mystylesheet.css">
</head>
```

Control

You can set leading (the space between lines of text) and word spacing, variables that are impossible to change using HTML. CSS also sets up items like drop caps (large, decorative capital letters at the start of a chapter) automatically, which in HTML you can do only by creating additional graphics. Designers can also position an element to appear anywhere on the screen and set standard spacing rules for paragraphs and images.

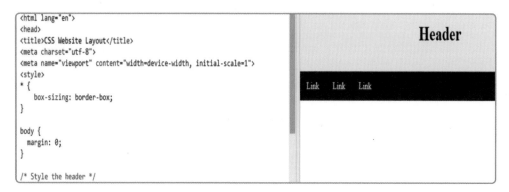

Above: You can adjust almost every aspect of a website's layout using CSS, including in this example the header and navigation bar.

CSS Styles

You can change almost every aspect of the styles and format of a website or web page (or indeed a single element), including:

➔ **Text**: Fonts, colours, styles such as bold or italics, and text size can all be changed using CSS.

➔ **Colours**: Background colours, margins, text boxes can all be assigned different colours.

➔ **Alignment**: You can align text, margins, borders, headers and footers using CSS.

➔ **Elements**: Things such as navigation buttons, drop-down menus, image borders and text boxes can all be altered using CSS.

INTERACTIVE FEATURES

You can use CSS to liven up your website and make it truly interactive for your viewers by adding interactive features such as hovering.

Hovering

CSS offers an easy way of highlighting text hyperlinks. Each CSS style you create has a property called 'hover', which is activated when the user places a cursor over a link. Alongside the definition of a style, you add a property called a:hover then specify the character traits you want changed when the cursor hovers, such as background colour and its value. You can even specify a different colour for a visited link using a:visited as the selector.

```
<style>
/* unvisited link */
a:link {
    color: green;
}

/* visited link */
a:visited {
    color: green;
}

/* mouse over link */
a:hover {
    color: red;
}

/* selected link */
a:active {
    color: yellow;
}
</style>
</head>
<body>
```

a:hover can change the colour of

Google.co.uk

Google.co.uk

Above: a:hover lets you change link colours when a mouse pointer hovers over them.

However, if you really want to delve into interactivity, you will need more than just CSS, so it is time to learn about scripts.

SCRIPTS

If you want to make your website interactive, you will need to know more than just HTML and CSS, and there are numerous different scripts available for the enthusiastic web designer.

WHAT IS A SCRIPT?

The distinction between programs and scripts is increasingly blurred. They both issue commands to tell the server (or browser) what to do. However, traditional programs are written in a heavyweight programming language such as C++, Java or Visual Basic, while scripts are written in the more specialized scripting languages such as Perl or JavaScript.

The scripts are run line by line through a script 'interpreter', which actions the commands. With web scripts, this interpreter is in the browser. By contrast, programs, which tend to be more complex, have to be compiled into machine code, which can be handled directly by the computer's processor.

```
<!DOCTYPE html>
<html>
<body>

<h2>JavaScript is a web script</h2>

<p id="demo">This script creates a button.</p>

<button type="button" onclick="myFunction()">Try it</button>

<p>(Web scripts are interpreted by the browser and actioned)</p>

<script src="myScript.js"></script>
```

JavaScript is a web script

This script creates a button.

[Try it]

(Web scripts are interpreted by the browser and actioned)

Above: Web scripts are interpreted by web browsers.

Web Scripts

Scripting languages tend to be more focused on the area in which they are used. So, for example, with JavaScript, which is designed purely for use on the Web, instructions centre on refining what the browser does, checking for plug-ins, browser versions and so on.

Using Scripts

As they are usually designed for a specific task, scripting languages are fairly easy to understand, even for complete novices. There are also many ready-made scripts freely available to download from the Web at sites like www.hotscripts.com. These cover both client-side scripting, such as JavaScript and server-side scripts like Perl.

Hot Tip

Scripts can be server-side, in that they sit on the website server, or they can be client-side and sit on the client, namely a web browser that is viewing your website.

Above: You can download ready-made scripts from websites such as www.hotscripts.com.

SERVER-SIDE SCRIPTS

Server-side scripts include:

➔ **PHP**: PHP: Hypertext Preprocessor (PHP) works in conjunction with MySQL databases and is used for installing interactive forums, blogging tools or a CMS to your web server.

➔ **PERL**: Practical Extraction and Report Language is good at processing text. It has become one of the most popular languages for writing Common Gateway Interface (CGI) scripts, particularly on UNIX machines.

➔ **ASP**: ASP is Microsoft's framework for server-side scripting and can handle major ecommerce sites or simple form-processing for those working with Windows-based web servers.

➔ **JSP**: Used for including a Java program as part of a web page to bring dynamic content to the Web.

CGI

To run a server-side script on a web server, the CGI protocol is used to communicate between a web server and an external program. CGI handles the flow of information. Scripts are CGI applications, and receive the data from the server and return it via the CGI. These programs are the most popular way for users to interact dynamically with a site, such as connecting to a database, sending information via email or processing information from a form.

PHP

By far the most commonly used, and the most useful, server-side script is PHP. PHP, an acronym for PHP: Hypertext Preprocessor, is open-source and free to download and use from the official PHP website (PHP.net).

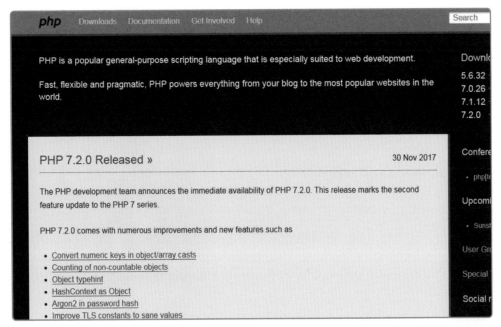

Above: You can download PHP from www.php.net as well as find useful resources and help in using the scripting language.

PHP Files

PHP files can contain text, HTML, CSS, JavaScript and PHP
code. All PHP code is executed on your web server and the
result is sent as plain HTML for the user's browser to
interpret. PHP files have extension '.php' and run on
various platforms, including Windows, Linux, Unix and
macOS. PHP also supports a wide range of databases. In
fact, the world's most popular content management system
(CMS), WordPress, is run on PHP, as is Facebook and a myriad of other websites.

Below: The PHP logo.

PHP can generate dynamic page content, collect form data, send and receive cookies and add,
delete and modify data in your database, as well as encrypting data.

A PHP file often contains HTML, and some PHP scripting, which starts with <?php and ends with ?>.

For example:

```
<!DOCTYPE html>
<html>
<body>

<h1>My PHP page</h1>

<?php
echo "This is PHP in action!";
?>

</body>
</html>
```

CLIENT-SIDE SCRIPTS

Client-side scripts are usually run on a browser. The processing takes place on the end user's computer (the client). The source code is transferred from the web server to the user's computer, but the scripting language needs to be enabled on the client computer first.

JAVASCRIPT

Below: The JavaScript logo.

JavaScript is perhaps the most common client-side scripting language. It is designed to bring some basic interactivity to web pages. It enables designers to control different elements. A scripting language such as JavaScript is somewhere between a mark-up language, such as HTML, and a fully fledged programming language, such as Java. The advantage of JavaScript is that it requires few programming skills and allows basic animation and special effects to be added to web pages.

Above: External JavaScript files have the extension .js.

Hot Tip

If you are using the same JavaScript code on different web pages, you can put it into an external script by writing it in a text editor and using the file extension .js.

Using JavaScript

The extra functionality JavaScript offers is added through short snippets of code that are written directly within the HTML code on a web page. It is enclosed within the `<script>` tag to tell the browser to run it as a JavaScript program; `<script>` tags can be placed in the `<head>` section, so the script can start running while the rest of the page is downloading, or in the `<body>` section if the script is used to write text to the screen.

JavaScript Interactivity

JavaScript can be used to add interactive elements to your HTML. It can be executed when needed and by using the `getElementById` tag you can attach it to specific HTML elements.

In the example below you can see how you can add a button to a page that changes the text on screen:

```
<!DOCTYPE html>
<html>
<body>

<h2> JavaScript Example</h2>

<p id="run">Click the button to change HTML content.</p>

<button type="button" onclick="document.getElementById('run').
innerHTML = 'This is JavaScript working'">Click</button>

</body>
</html>

<script>
```

JavaScript Example

Click the button to change HTML content.

Click

JavaScript Example

This is JavaScript working

Click

Above: This JavaScript example will change the text on screen when you click a button.

Writing JavaScript

Programs such as Adobe's Dreamweaver can do the JavaScript coding for you, but there are also sites where you can download ready-made scripts to add to your page, such as the JavaScript source (www.javascriptsource.com).

VBSCRIPT

Visual Basic Script Edition is a client-side scripting language, similar to JavaScript. VBScript is based on Microsoft's Visual Basic programming language, although it is simpler to use. It is embedded in the HTML file in the `<head>` of the document, so the script is loaded into the memory while the rest of the page is downloading. The script will run as it is read – if, for example, it is checking which version of a browser is being used – or on some event, such as a click of the mouse or a rollover.

Trouble with Redis?

HOME   ABOUT   FAQ   FORUM   CORE REFERENCE   NEWSLETTER

Categories
▸ Alphabetical Listing
▸ Tutorials
▸ Ajax Tutorials
▸ Ajax
▸ Buttons
▸ Cookies
▸ CSS
▸ Forms
▸ Games
▸ Generators
▸ Image Effects
▸ Math Related

The JavaScript Source is an excellent JavaScript resource with tons of "cut and paste" JavaScript examples for your Web pages. All for free!

Featured Scripts from JavaScript Source

FreeFallMenu by Maciej Plesnar
  Maciej Ple??nar

Cool drop-down 3d menu effect with real physics in css and javascript. Read More

Show Current Date/Time on Web Page by Zyvxn
  Zyvxn

This script shows you the simple code to display the current date on your Web page. Read More

JavaScript: Building a fitness app – data and models (Article)

Follow the first few steps of building a fitness app using JavaScript. Read More

Palindrome Checker by muazzam

Above: Ready-made JavaScripts can be found at www.javascriptsource.com.

USING DYNAMIC CONTENT

Not all web browsers support all scripts. For instance, VBScript, which allows web designers to provide dynamic content such as interactive navigational controls, is only supported by Microsoft's Internet Explorer browser, and not Firefox or Chrome, which only support JavaScript. Similarly, most browsers have a security function that allows users to turn off scripting, which means there is no guarantee that your client-side scripting is supported by your website's visitors.

> **Hot Tip**
>
> Consider providing alternative content for users whose web browsers do not allow particular scripts. You can do this using the `<noscript>` and `</noscript>` tags.

Above: Not all web browsers support all scripts.

FLASH

Adobe's Flash is a software technology for creating and managing interactive multimedia web applications such as animations, movies, games, advertisement banners and more. Many web designers use Flash to liven up their web pages and bring an extra dimension to content.

Using Flash

It is worth knowing that Flash animations can be placed on the page using the `<object>` and `<embed>` tags. The former defines the size and name of a movie and the version of Flash that was used to create it; the `<embed>` tag includes its display attributes and the filename and location of the movie. You can set height, width and alignment, and specify the amount of white space to leave around the object.

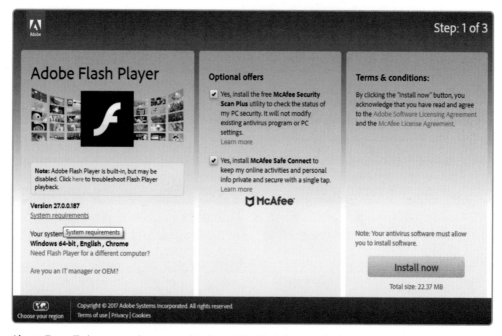

Above: To run Flash content, a browser needs to have Adobe Flash Player installed.

OTHER WEB LANGUAGES

There are so many web languages around today that it would be impossible to include them all in this book, but here are just a few of the other languages that it may be useful to have some knowledge of.

XML

Extensible Markup Language (XML) is similar to HTML in syntax, but operates differently. While HTML controls how documents are displayed, XML simply looks at the structure. It separates the content on a page from the way it is presented. As a mark-up language, HTML uses a fixed number of tags; it also specifies exactly what each one means and how it will look in the browser. XML only uses the tags to separate pieces of data. So, <p> in an XML file is not necessarily a paragraph mark, but can be anything – such as a price or person – according to the application that reads it.

With XML, users create their own tags for special kinds of documents, such as a medical chart or a transcript of a play. XML-capable browsers then lay out the document following instructions supplied in the associated style sheets.

```
<breakfast_menu>
  <food>
     <name>Belgian Waffles</name>
     <price>$5.95</price>
     <description>Two of our famous Belgian Waffles with plenty of real maple syrup</description>
     <calories>650</calories> </food>
  <food>
     <name>Strawberry Belgian Waffles</name>
     <price>$7.95</price>
     <description>Light Belgian waffles covered with strawberries and whipped cream</description>
     <calories>900</calories> </food>
  <food>
     <name>Berry-Berry Belgian Waffles</name>
     <price>$8.95</price>
     <description>Light Belgian waffles covered with an assortment of fresh berries and whipped cream</descripti
     <calories>900</calories> </food>
  <food>
     <name>French Toast</name>
     <price>$4.50</price>
     <description>Thick slices made from our homemade sourdough bread</description>
     <calories>600</calories> </food>
  <food>
     <name>Homestyle Breakfast</name>
     <price>$6.95</price>
     <description>Two eggs, bacon or sausage, toast, and our ever-popular hash browns</description>
     <calories>950</calories> </food>
</breakfast_menu>
```

Above: An example XML file used to create a breakfast menu from ww.w3schools.com.

XHTML

Almost identical to HTML, Extensible Hypertext Markup Language (XHMTL) is slightly stricter and is defined as an XML application. Essentially, it is HTML but with XML syntax. XHTML was specifically designed for smaller handheld devices and is more precise and predictable than HTML. However, HTML5 has now made XHTML all but obsolete.

DHTML

Dynamic HTML (DHTML) is a collection of technologies that, when combined, can be used to make traditional static web pages dynamic. DHTML uses HTML plus, client-side scripting languages, such as JavaScript, and presentation languages, such as CSS. The aim of DHTML is to take the ordinary text-and-graphics web page and bring it to life. As no plug-ins are required with DHTML, files are small, which are quicker to download than graphics files, and render faster than alternatives such as Flash.

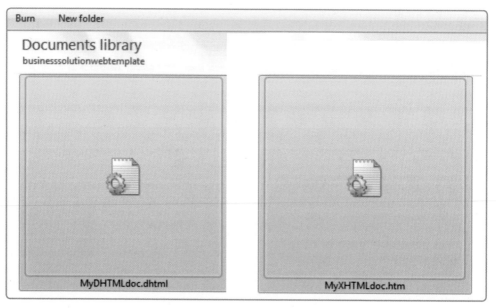

Above: DHTML has the file extension .dhtml but XHTML uses .html (or htm) because it is just HTML with XML syntax.

Java

Java was originally designed as a programming language and operating system for the consumer electronics market, to control everything from TV sets to toasters. Although it did not succeed there, it had a number of features that made it ideal for the Web. It is small (as it was designed to fit into items with little memory), can be transferred quickly and is platform-independent. Java is mainly used on the Web to create applets – which can be embedded on a page. These programs, which have the extension .class, can add all sorts of interactive features to a site.

Above: The Java logo.

Jargon Buster

An applet is a program that is launched from HTML to run in a web browser, providing web applications with interactive features that HTML cannot normally provide.

ActiveX Controls

ActiveX controls can add greater interactivity to web pages than other technologies, but you

Above: The ActiveX logo.

should bear in mind that they also carry greater risks. ActiveX is the brand name of a group of technologies developed by Microsoft, which sets down rules for how applications share information. ActiveX programs – called controls – are reusable bits of software that add interactivity to a web page. Though ActiveX is not actually a language, these mini programs are similar to Java applets.

The controls are downloaded to your hard drive, where they are saved. This means that, if you visit a page which needs the same control, it will not be downloaded again. Once downloaded, ActiveX controls can access all parts of your computer, which means they carry a greater security risk than, say, Java applets.

CONTENT MANAGEMENT SYSTEMS

Content Management Systems can take a lot of the headache out of web design. A CMS enables you to control the content for your web page, add pages and elements, and reduce the need to write separate code for each page.

CMS

Good writers with equally good web programming skills are a rare breed, so online publishers and other companies where a lot of people produce a lot of pages for the same site use a content management system (CMS) to upload words and pictures. Companies often have their CMS custom-built but, in recent years, web content management systems have been made available online for personal and corporate use.

Below: WordPress is one of the most widely used CMS systems.

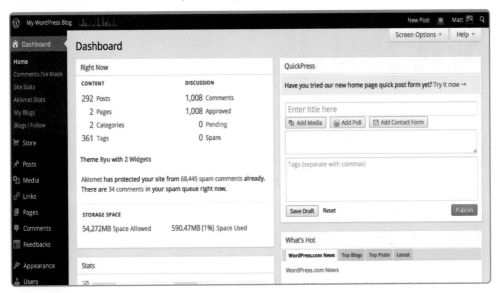

Database

Content Management Systems tend to use databases (often MySQL). Their purpose is to create, edit and store HTML content so you can manage it easily. Content Management Systems usually have some sort of portal, known as the 'back end' that lets you add content and make changes. The website managed by the CMS that visitors see is called the 'front end'.

Jargon Buster

MySQL is a database system used for web applications. It is ideal for managing large amounts of data and is the backbone behind large websites such as Twitter and YouTube.

Below: The MySQL logo.

WHY A CMS?

If you have a very large website, or one that you want to add to frequently, such as a blog connected to your website, then a CMS can save vast amounts of time, as new content can be added quickly, while changes to pages are simple to make.

CHOOSING A CMS

There are many CMS available on the Web for you to use. Some are free to use, others cost money, but the important thing is to find the right CMS for your needs.

Some things to look out for:

 Hosting: Your web host needs to be able to accommodate your CMS, as it will have to run on your web server.

➔ **Installation:** You want something quick and easy to install.

➔ **Ease of use**: CMS range from simple, easy-to-use portals to very complicated management systems.

➔ **Support:** Many content management systems have large user communities from whom you can draw support and assistance.

WORDPRESS

The daddy of all content management systems, WordPress started life as a blogging platform, but its ease of use, large support community and ability to handle all sorts of files and elements meant it soon became adopted by web developers. Indeed, developers do not just

Above: The WordPress homepage.

Hot Tip

WordPress has its own hosting platform, www.wordpress.com. This has the same administrative interface but will host your blog or website for you too.

use WordPress to manage their web content, but many web designers use its WYSIWYG administrative interface to create websites and web pages. Thousands of website templates have been created for WordPress and it is perhaps the most widely supported CMS available.

WordPress is open-source and available to download at www.wordpress.org.

JOOMLA!

Another popular CMS, Joomla!, lets you create and manage websites using a simple interface not dissimilar from the forms-based blog front end. Once you have created your structure of

Above: Welcome to Joomla!

sections and menu items (and this should be set out in advance just like a home-coded site), a wide community of developers is constantly developing plug-in modules, such as polls and galleries, that you can add to your site. Some of these will cost money but many others are free. The same community is usually on hand to answer your queries on any aspect of the system. Designers are also hard at work creating templates of all colours and styles for you to incorporate into your site. You can download the Joomla! software from www.joomla.org.

Hot Tip

Other CMS packages are available, such as the self-explanatory CMS Made Simple (www.cmsmadesimple.org). Most good CMS packages will also help your site's searchability with Google-friendly URLs and correctly assigned <meta> tags.

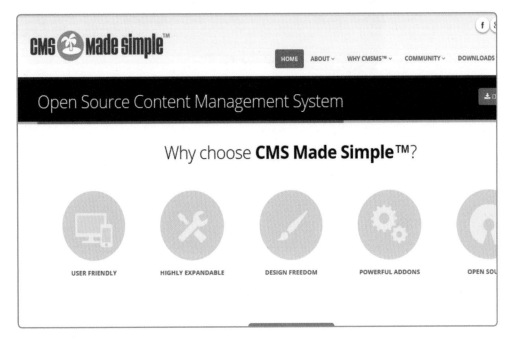

Above: CMS Made Simple.

ADDING TO YOUR WEBSITE

USEFUL PAGES

You may have created a homepage, an about page, a contact page and several other pages, but there are many other useful pages you can add to a website to improve a user's experience.

LANDING PAGE

You may think you have it all covered. You have created a well-structured website, with every web page easy to navigate from the homepage. However, how do you know your visitors will arrive at your homepage first? The difficulty with web visitors is they can land anywhere on

Above: Landing pages often have a specific purpose.

your website depending on various factors, such as what they entered into a search engine, or whether they responded on a pay-per-click advertisement (see more on this later in this chapter). To get around this, many web designers introduce landing pages to their website.

WHAT IS A LANDING PAGE?

In short, a landing page is any web page that a visitor lands on when they first visit your website. However, many web designers create specific landing pages to funnel visitors who have come from a particular location, most often from an advertising link. In this sense, a landing page is a standalone web page distinct from the main website that has a specific purpose, such as encouraging a visitor to make a purchase. Landing pages come in two different types: click-through and lead-generation.

Above: Click-through landing pages often have a call to action (CTA).

Click-Through Landing Pages

These encourage visitors to click through to another page. In an ecommerce environment, they are often sales pages that describe a product and encourage visitors to make a purchase and click through to a cart or payment page.

Lead-Generation Landing Pages

These are designed to capture data from a visitor, such as a name or email address, which will allow you to market to that specific visitor. These lead-generation pages are often in the guise of a form, along with an inducement to provide information, such as a free gift, a white paper, discount voucher, a regular newsletter or entry into a competition.

Above: Forms, such as Facebook's sign-up form, enable you to obtain information from visitors.

CREATING FORMS

Forms are an ideal way to receive feedback or request information on landing pages. In HTML, forms are set up with the `<form>...</form>` tags. Within the opening tag, you need to specify the 'action' attribute (the address of the program that will process the form) and the 'method' attribute (which specifies how the information will be sent).

Form Coding

For a feedback form, you will probably want a text input field where visitors put specific information, such as their name, as well as a text box where they add general comments. For single-line text, use the `<input>` tag with the attribute type="text". You can control the length of the visible field by using the 'size' attribute. To limit the number of characters users can enter, add the 'maxlength' attribute.

The <textarea> tag creates a text box for free-flowing comment. The visible size is set with the 'rows' and 'cols' attributes. For example, <textarea name="feedback" rows="4" cols="25">...</textarea> would create a box that would take four lines of text with 25 characters in a line. Any more than that and the box would scroll.

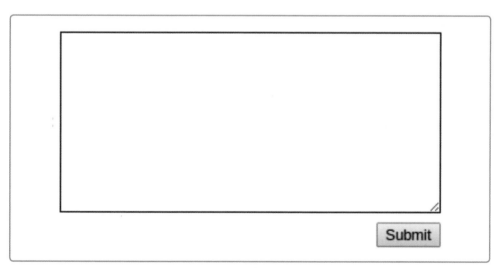

Above: The <textarea> tag creates a text box for comments and messages.

If you want to prompt people about what details to include, add some text between the opening and closing `<textarea>` tags.

To round off the form, add a submit button, created by using the `<input>` tag and putting 'submit' as the attribute. Clicking this will send the form information to the URL previously set in the 'action' attribute.

Form Fields

Form fields are the areas on a form where users enter requested information (such as on a feedback form or any other page where a user must fill in information). The most common method will be through a text field, where visitors are prompted to enter details, such as a name or address. Where longer comments are needed, a text-box field can be added. Selection-type form fields such as check boxes, radio buttons and drop-down menus are also used to gather information.

Your E-mail

ex: myname@example.com

Text Box

Text Area

Above: Form fields are text boxes that can request all sorts of information, such as email addresses, names and other details.

Form Handling

This is the processing and interpreting of data from HTML forms. The best-looking forms are worthless unless you have some way of accessing and manipulating the information entered. Form handlers are separate scripts that take this information and process it.

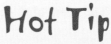

Hot Tip

The simplest form handler is built into HTML. The 'mailto:' form simply takes the information a user enters and sends it to a specified email address.

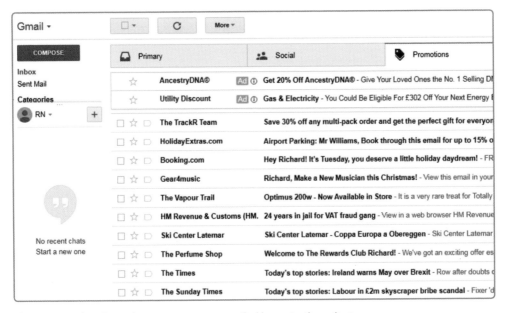

Above: You can have form information sent to your email address using the mailto: tag.

For a simple form, it may be possible to use JavaScript or some other client-side scripting to analyse the form and return the values. Otherwise, the users' responses need to be sent to an email address or to a server-side application, typically CGI or ASP (CGI scripts that handle simple forms are freely available on the Web).

Thank You

We have received your information.

 <u>Click here</u> to return to the site.

Above: Place a link on a confirmation page to take a visitor back to the main website.

COOKIES

Information entered on a website, such as on a form, can be saved for future use using cookies. Cookies are small data files stored on a browser to remember certain information whenever you visit a specific website. For instance, if you have to log in to a website, a cookie can store your username and password to prevent you from having to submit them during every visit. Generally, cookies are written in JavaScript, and you can find ready-made cookie scripts online.

Cookies are created using the 'document.cookie' property and are saved in name-value pairs such as:

```
document.cookie = "username = John Smith";
```

SITEMAPS

Sitemaps are an overview of the site structure, designed to help users find their way around your website.

Setting up a Sitemap

Sitemaps are ideal for large websites or those with complicated structures. Sitemaps are just like indexes or tables of contents in books. To save on download time, it is usually easier to use a text-based sitemap rather than a graphical one. Setting it within a table makes it easier to format (for more on tables see the next section). Sitemaps also aid search-engine placement, as it makes it easier for the search-engine spiders to discover all your pages.

There are three types of sitemap:

→ **Indexed sitemap**: A directory or an alphabetical listing of your site's pages.

→ **Complete categorical sitemap**: A comprehensive sitemap with links classified into categories.

→ **Restricted categorical**: Links in a specific category are displayed but individual pages are not linked in the sitemap.

Search Guides	Services	Tools	Help Centers
• Basics of Search	• Alerts	• Maps	
• Advanced Search	• Answers	• Mobile	
• Search Results Page	• Catalogs	• News Search	
• Setting Preferences	• Directory	• Scholar	
• Search Features	• Froogle	• Special Searches	
• Services & Tools	• Groups	• University Search	
• Help Center	• Google Apps	• Web Search	
	• Images		
	• Google Labs		
	• Local		

Corporate Overview	Investor Relations	Press Center	Hiring
• Company	• Financial Info	• Media Resources	• U.S. Jobs
• Features	• Financial Data	• News from Google	• International Jobs
• Technology	• News & Events	• Images and B-roll	• Benefits

Above: Sitemaps contain links to all your main categories or web pages.

DYNAMIC STRUCTURE

A variety of techniques can vastly improve the visitor experience and give you more control over your website layout. Using tables and adding dynamic navigation tools can also make your website much easier for your visitors to get around.

PRICING TABLE TEMPLATE

PLANS	START	PRO	ULTIMATE
PRICING TABLE	$5.99 per month	$8.99 per month	$10.99 per month
DESCRIPTION#1	✔	✔	✔
DESCRIPTION#2	�’	✔	✔
DESCRIPTION#3	✗	✗	✔
DESCRIPTION#4	✗	✗	✔
DESCRIPTION#5	✗	✔	✔
DESCRIPTION#6	✗	✗	✔
	BUY NOW	BUY NOW	BUY NOW

Above: Tables can be a good way of structuring your web page's content.

TABLES

Tables offer a good way to clearly structure the page layout and are useful for controlling alignment, to ensure your web page always looks the way you want it to. For the overall page structure, tables can be used to create the major sections. For instance, a left-hand column could house the navigation buttons, while the main column has the content. The width of the table can either be fixed (each column is a precise number of pixels) or relative (where they are resized relative to the width of the window).

Using Tables

Table width is set to 100 per cent and each column is a percentage of this. Tables can also be a combination of fixed and relative values. For example, the left-hand navigation is set to a fixed pixel width, while the main content section varies as the window is resized.

Tables are made up from the `<table>`...`</table>` tags with rows inside `<tr>`...`</tr>`. Inside each row are the table cells `<td>`...`</td>` marked for table data. These are where the content – either text or graphics – goes. There are no column tags; the number of columns is measured by the number of `<td>` tags within each row.

To avoid a rigid block design, you can stretch cells so that they span a number of rows or columns. Spanning is controlled by the 'rowspan' and 'colspan' attributes.

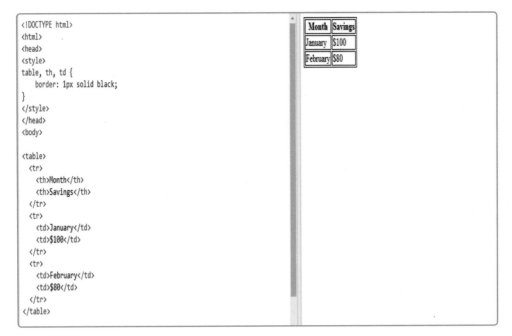

Above: Table tags define the size and span of a table. The <th> tag can be used to place headers in tables.

For example, in a two-column table, you could stretch the top row of cells across one column to create space for a heading (for example `<td colspan="2">Heading</td>`).

Manipulating Tables

Aside from using the table to format the page, there are attributes that let you format the appearance of the table. Elements you control at the table level (that is, with the `<table>` tag) are the width and height of the table, the spacing between cells ('cellspacing' attribute), the padding within cells ('cellpadding' attribute), the border thickness ('border') and background colour ('bgcolor'). While you are constructing the table, it is easiest to set the border to 1 so it is visible. At the cell level, you can alter the width and height of cells, the background colour and the alignment of objects.

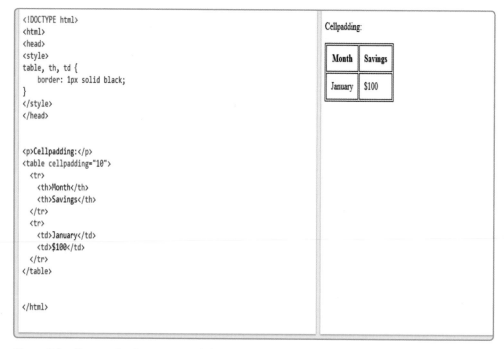

```
<!DOCTYPE html>
<html>
<head>
<style>
table, th, td {
    border: 1px solid black;
}
</style>
</head>

<p>Cellpadding:</p>
<table cellpadding="10">
    <tr>
        <th>Month</th>
        <th>Savings</th>
    </tr>
    <tr>
        <td>January</td>
        <td>$100</td>
    </tr>
</table>

</html>
```

Cellpadding:

Month	Savings
January	$100

Above: Cellpadding specifies the space, in pixels, between the cell wall and the cell content.

DYNAMIC NAVIGATION

Dynamic navigation, where menu items break out of the static to offer more options or simply to emphasize interactivity, livens up a website, engages the reader and offers a convenient way to make the most of limited screen space.

Rollovers

The simplest form of dynamic navigation device is a rollover; a change of colour or image when a mouse hovers over a button draws the reader's attention to a link. Browsers highlight text and graphical hyperlinks by changing the cursor from a conventional pointer to a hand symbol but, if you want links and buttons to be absolutely clear to readers, visual triggers are key, and changing the state of a graphical or text hyperlink is simple and effective.

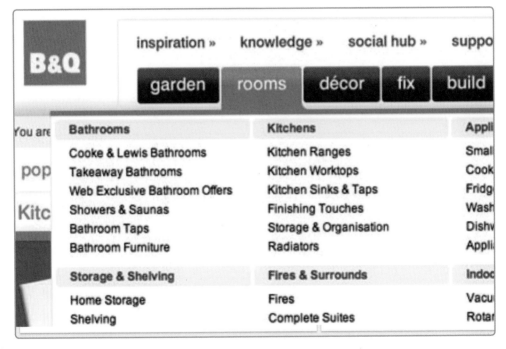

Above: Dynamic navigation such as on this B&Q website adds extra interactivity to web menus.

Types of Rollover

There are three main types of rollover:

⊖ **Button rollovers**: Where an image changes as the cursor hovers over it.

Above: One of the most common rollovers is when a mouse pointer turns into the hand icon when you hover over a button.

⊖ **Distance (or disjointed) rollovers**: Where a remote image changes as you hover over a series of buttons.

⊖ **One-to-many rollovers**: A combination of the two.

Button rollovers are the most common, and are usually used for menu items and hyperlinks. Distance and one-to-many rollovers are widely used on homepages, where the user might hover over a menu item and see a written explanation of that section of the site elsewhere on screen.

Drop-Down Menus

Dynamic drop-down menus can be great space-saving devices. If your site is divided into 30 sections, it is impossible to run a horizontal menu across the screen, and impractical to run a lengthy menu down the side of the page. Instead, you can group the sections under a few main menu headings, which, when hovered over or clicked on, call up a menu containing the sub-sections, just like application menus.

The easiest and cleanest way to do this is through CSS. By using nested list tags, you can add fly-outs to your drop-down menus so third-tier menu items appear on the right of the items on a drop-down menu. It is a great way of simplifying navigation on complex sites without forcing the user to drill down on page after page until they find what they want.

Above: Dynamic menus, such as on this web design website, give you sub-menus when you click or hover.

JavaScript Menus

JavaScript menus aren't necessary, but a combination of CSS and JavaScript can add additional features like time-out, so if a user hovers for too long, the menu will close. You can find ready-made JavaScript menu generators online.

FIXED-WIDTH PAGE DESIGN

If your website has lots of elements on the page and you want it to display a certain way, you may want to fix the page width. However, you have no way of predicting the size of the screen and the browser that a visitor will be using, so setting a fixed-width page design can result in short columns of text stretching across or smaller graphics disappearing across the wide expanse when viewed on a large screen. Conversely, on mobile devices large graphics can dominate to the detriment of the words, menus and other page elements.

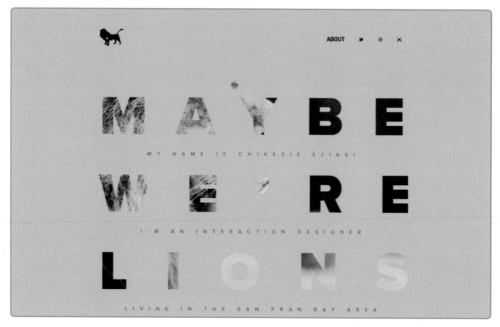

Above: A fixed-width page design lets you use interesting effects, such as on this web design website, but it should be used with care.

Mobile Versions

You can reduce the risk of large graphics dominating by designing pages to a set width and having separate websites for larger screens and mobile devices. If you choose to do this and have a fixed-width design, you must ensure your website works on the lowest common denominator. For a website that runs on a computer, 1024 x 768 is generally the smallest resolution used these days (although a fraction of users may be using smaller resolution).

You can use a PHP script for detecting mobile devices such as http://mobiledetect.net.

A better solution may be to write a media-query based CSS file for resolutions that are common to smartphones. This avoids the need for browser detection and a separate mobile-friendly site.

For example:

```
<link rel='stylesheet' media='screen
and (min-width: 701px) and (max-
width: 900px)' href='css/medium.css
```

Viewport

With the introduction of HTML5, web designers now have control over the viewport via the `<meta>` tag. A viewport essentially instructs a browser how to scale a website to fit a mobile device and this is by far a better solution than trying to fix page widths.

To control viewport, use the following:

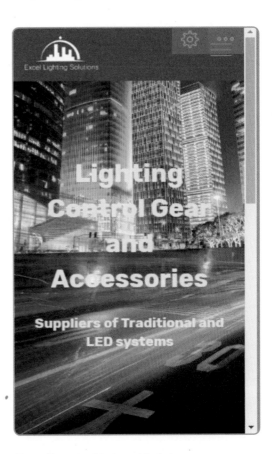

Above: If you can detect a mobile device you can use a fixed-width design to fit both PC and mobile versions.

```
<meta name="viewport" content="width=device-width,
initial-scale=1.0">
```

The width=device-width sets the width of the page to match the width of the device's screen. The initial-scale=1.0 sets the zoom level when the page is loaded by the browser.

Above: The viewport is the amount of web page you can see in your browser, which may depend on how large your browser window is.

OPENING NEW WINDOWS

If you are linking to external websites, the last thing you want is for a user to disappear, never to return. You can avoid this by opening up a link in a new tab or new browser window. You can tell a browser to open an external link in a new browser tab or window by adding a target="_blank" attribute to your links.

For example, rather than having a link and anchor text such as:

```
<a href="https://www.externalwebsite.
com/">External website link</a>
```

Add the target="_blank" after the link's URL:

```
<a href="https://www. externalwebsite.
com/" target="_blank"> External
website link</a>
```

Hot Tip

Whether a link opens up in a new window or new tab using the target="_blank" attribute will depend on the browser being used and how it is set up.

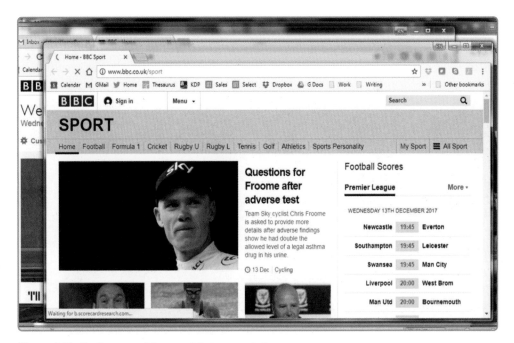

Above: ="_blank" will open any link a user clicks in a new window.

DYNAMIC CONTENT

Animations, videos and certain advanced graphics techniques can create dynamic effects on the page and really add some oomph to your website.

MULTIMEDIA

Nothing brings a page alive more than the use of multimedia. Animations, animated gifs and video can turn a static website into a dynamic, immersive user experience, but you need to use them with caution.

VIDEO

Back when the Web was in its infancy, videos were a rare commodity on websites, primarily because video files are very large and older computers with slow connections would struggle to load them. These days, the Web is awash with video. Indeed, online TV networks such as Netflix, Amazon Video and Now TV are as popular for watching TV and films as regular TV channels.

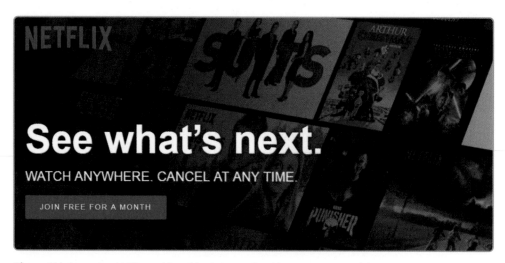

Above: Websites such as Netflix provide nothing but streaming video content onto web browsers.

Adding Video Content

Of course, video files remain large. An entire movie, for instance, could be as big as 1 GB (1000 MB), and nobody wants to wait ten minutes for a website to load because it contains a massive video file. However, there are far more efficient and practical ways to add video content to a website.

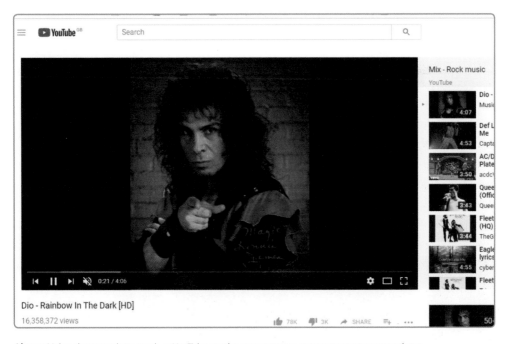

Above: Video-sharing websites such as YouTube are the easiest way to get content onto your website.

🡢 **Embedding video**: The easiest way to install video on your website is to embed it from websites such as YouTube.

🡢 **Streaming**: Content delivery networks, such as Onstream Media, will host and stream your videos to your website.

➔ **Web hosting**: You can stream a
video direct from your web host
server, but this does take storage
and bandwidth. You will also need
to install a video player, such as
Adobe Flash, Apple Quicktime or
Windows Media Player.

Jargon Buster
**Streaming is a method of using a
continuous stream of data to watch video
in real time rather than downloading the
entire file to your computer.**

EMBEDDING YOUTUBE VIDEOS

Because it is so easy, the go-to method for nearly all web developers wanting to host a video
on a website is to upload it to YouTube. The video site will host the video, so it costs you
nothing in storage and bandwidth, but users can watch it on your web page.

1.   Go to the YouTube video you want to embed and under the video, click the 'share' button.

2.   Click 'Embed'.

Step 2. Clicking 'Embed'.

3. A box appears with HTML code. Copy and paste the code into your website's HTML.

Step 3. The embedded video code.

You can adjust the size of the video on your website using the `<iframe>` element:

```
<iframe width="420" height="315"
src="https://www.youtube.com/embed/
XGSy3_Czz8k">
</iframe>
```

HTML5 Video

For many years, the most common technology powering web-based video was Adobe Flash. Even YouTube was until recently only Adobe Flash-based. However, as some devices (namely Apple iPhones and tablets) were released without Flash support

Hot Tip

You can have your video play automatically (as opposed to a user clicking play) when a user visits your web page, by adding: ?autoplay=1 to the YouTube link, but be warned, people may find this annoying.

(to play a Flash-based video, a user needs Flash player installed in their browser), HTML5 is now catching up with Flash's popularity.

ANIMATED GIFS

Animated GIFs are graphic images that move. Essentially, these are a string of images that are displayed one after the other, much like a flick-book where separate images appear to move when the pages are quickly flicked through. As such, GIFs are a great way to display multiple images in a single pane, or small animation/video files.

Above: Animated GIFs use separate images displayed one after the other, so that they move.

Creating GIFs

Creating GIFs is quite easy. You can upload your own images to Photoshop using the: File > Scripts > Load Files Into Stack, option, and saving the stack as a GIF, but websites such as GIFMaker.me (http://gifmaker.me/) will do the same thing and are much quicker and easier to use. Obviously, if you want to adjust images before you create your GIF, then Photoshop may be the best option.

Hot Tip

You can put a large image or GIF file on the homepage and set the 'width' and 'height' attributes to one pixel so it will be all but invisible, but when the user goes to the page where the image is full size, it will be loaded instantly from the image cache.

Otherwise you can upload your images to a website such as GIFMaker.me, create your GIF, and then place it in your website as you would with any other image file.

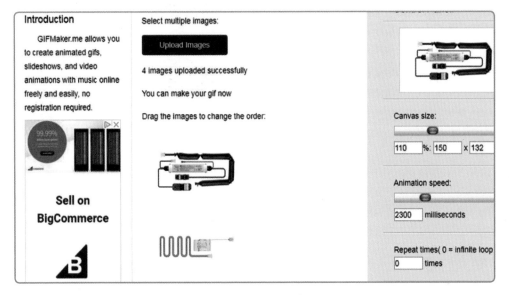

Above: Websites such as GIFMaker.me make it easy to create animated GIFs.

GRAPHICS

No matter what font you use, plain text in your headings can come across as a little staid, while square images in a frame can also be a little dull. Thankfully, you can employ a number of techniques to add a little spice to your text, images and other elements.

Anti-Aliasing

Because everything shown on screen is mapped to square pixels, the edges of curved lines in images and text will have a block effect. Images like this are said to be aliased. Imaging programs, such as Photoshop, enable you to anti-alias graphics by blending the edges with tints of the next colour to smooth over the jagged lines.

Effects

Effects such as drop shadows, glows and bevels can be added, and you can fill bold text with a pattern or a graduated tint. Textures, combined with colour and lighting, can also be used to enhance the appearance of embossed elements. Brown-tinted embossed text or line-art on a wooden texture can look like a carving, while a metal textured image can resemble a coin or engraved metal nameplate.

Above: Anti-aliasing blurs or smooths the edges of text or images.

Using bevelling effects adds raised edges to buttons and other small geometric shapes, giving a 3D effect. Different looks can be created by using an outer bevel (which makes the whole object look raised) or inner (which applies a raised and textured border).

IMAGE SATURATION AND HUE

For images, altering the hue and saturation increases the tone and intensity. Every image has a subtle underlying colour, and if it is incorrect – skin tones might have a blue tint, for instance – tweaking the hue can correct it. Saturation refers to the volume of colour in an image. If an image looks cold and colourless, increasing the saturation gives warmth.

Hot Tip

A shadow effect added to text, a background, photo or button can give the impression of depth. Most photo editors work in similar ways: select the graphic and apply the shadow effect.

SHADOW

Above: Shadows add depth to text.

SOCIAL MEDIA, SEO AND BLOGS

You may have designed and created the greatest website, but it will all be for nothing if you get no visitors. Getting people to your website requires taking advantage of social media networks, blogging and ensuring your web pages are optimized for search engines.

SOCIAL MEDIA

The rise of social media has changed the way people use the Internet. A social media presence can drive traffic to your website and, increasingly, people are using social media to find content and websites, rather than just relying on traditional search engines. This makes a social media presence important for any website intent on getting traffic.

Social Media Buttons

One of the best ways to ensure a social media presence is to encourage the sharing of your web content, and the simplest way to do this is with social media buttons.

Above: Social media buttons such as on this blog make it easy for visitors to share your content.

To add social media buttons to your website, you have two options:

➔ **Catchall**: A service such as ShareThis (www.sharethis.com) or AddToAny (www.addtoany. com) will generate the code for a social media interface for you to place on your site.

➔ **Individual**: You can get the code for individual buttons from social media sites such as Facebook and Twittter.

Adding a Twitter Button

Most social media sites have a simple method of generating the code for your sharing buttons. For instance, this is how to add a Twitter button:

Hot Tip

Include your sharing button at the top of your web pages so that it is visible as soon as the page loads and no scrolling is required.

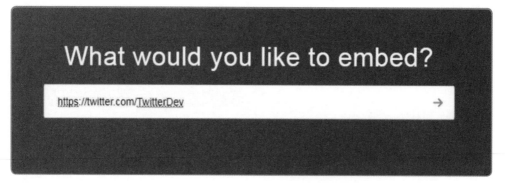

What would you like to embed?

https://twitter.com/TwitterDev

Step 2. A Twitter button of your profile will make it easy for visitors on your website to follow you on Twitter.

1.   Log in to your Twitter account and go to https://publish.twitter.com/

2.   Customize the 'Follow' button to your liking with the available options, such as your Twitter profile.

3.   Choose your button and copy and paste the code into the HTML of your website.

That's all we need, unless you'd like to set customization options.

By embedding Twitter content in your website or app, you are agreeing to the Developer Agreement and Developer Policy.

`<a href="https://twitter.com/TwitterDev?ref_src=twsrc%5Etfw" class="twitter-follow-button" data-show-count="f`   Copy Code

Follow @TwitterDev

Step 3. Copying the HTML code for your Twitter button.

SEO FRIENDLY

Search Engine Optimization is crucial to people finding your website on Google and other search engines. Along with ensuring you have the correct meta data in your HTML, there are other steps you can take to ensure an optimized website.

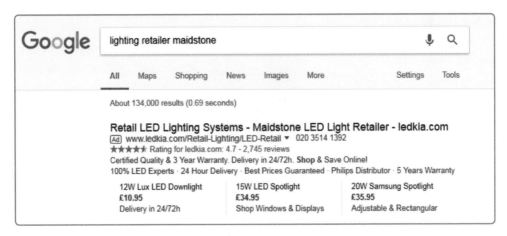

Above: If you want visitors to find your website on search engines you need to make sure it is SEO friendly.

Keywords: Make sure your content reflects what your website is about. A good way to do this is to ensure relevant keywords appear in the text.

Structure: Your website needs to be easy to navigate for search-engine spiders and quick to load.

> ## Hot Tip
>
> **Register your website with Google and Bing webmaster tools. Once you have registered, you will get notified if there is a problem with your website and receive useful statistics.**

Links: Inbound links from trusted, authoritative websites can help you rise up the rankings, so think about a link-building campaign.

Content: Content needs to be useful, relevant and fresh. Regularly adding new content is one easy way of doing this.

BLOGGING

Blogging is a great way to encourage social media shares as well as ensuring you have regular fresh content on your website. Blogging is also a great way to encourage people to visit your website, as you are offering visitors something for nothing. You can also generate a lot of inbound links by blogging.

THOUSANDS OF BEAUTIFUL LIGHTS

If you love what you see and want to see more, visit our web store now!

Lights; They're Not Just for Chr

📅 December 7, 2017   👤 Karen Hill

Wish it could be Christmas every day yourself to some beautiful chandelie home lighting you can enjoy all year

Above: Blogs are a good way of ensuring your website has plenty of regular, new content.

Blogging can be fun, but it does take some commitment and you may need to install a CMS on your web server in order to manage and add new content. Ideally, a blog should be connected to your main website in a sub-domain, such as www.mywebsite.com/blog.

BUSINESS WEBSITES

Business websites have different needs to regular websites. If you want to create an e-commerce website and take payments online, or run an advertising campaign, this doesn't have to be difficult or expensive.

E-COMMERCE

The Web is not just a place where businesses can advertise their products and services. Websites now can handle all aspects of e-commerce, from taking payments to arranging shipping. If you want to create an e-commerce website, you will need an e-commerce platform that can handle payments, and there are plenty available to choose from.

➔ **3dcart**: www.3dcart.co.uk. Can be used as a complete storefront but will also allow you to import your existing web design (prices start from $19.99/£21 a month).

Selling online should be as easy as shopping

3dcart has everything you need to build your online store; from real-time shipping to your choice of payments. Increase visitors and sales with the best ecommerce platform for SEO.

Start your 15-Day FREE Trial. No credit card required.

| Email Address | Let's Get Started |

Launch a Mobile-Ready Online Store

Market your store within one platform

ANGEL FASHION

HOME

Categories

TOPS
ACTIVATED
SHIRTS
DRESSES
JEANS
ACCESSORIES

Above: Shopping cart software such as 3dcart will let you import your web design onto their e-commerce platform.

- **Shopify:** www.shopify.com. Will handle all the hosting, security and payment processing for you for a monthly fee (from $14/£10 per month).

- **Opencart:** www.opencart.com. A free (open-source) e-commerce solution that can be easily customized.

ADVERTISING YOUR WEBSITE

Businesses can also take advantage of online advertising from places such as Google AdWords (https://adwords.google.com) and Yahoo Advertising (https://advertising.yahoo.com). These usually charge on a pay-per-click (PPC) basis. PPC advertising is usually fairly simple to set up:

1. Set your budget per day.

2. Set the geographical location in which you want your ads to show.

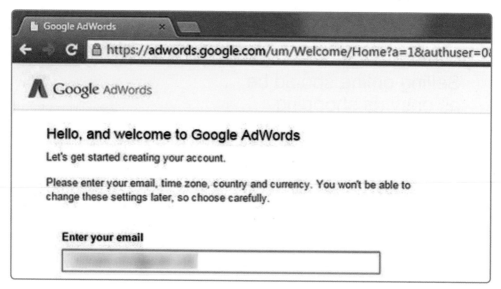

Above: Google AdWords is very easy to set up: just answer the relevant questions about your website, location and budget.

3.   Choose to display advertising on search results or on websites that host adverts.

4.   Choose the keywords that will trigger the display of your advert.

MONETIZING YOUR WEBSITE

Even if you are not an e-commerce website, you can still make money online by displaying adverts on your website. You can do this in a number of ways.

⊕   **AdSense**: Google's AdSense (www.google.co.uk/adsense) and Bing/Yahoo's Media.net (www.media.net) let you place PPC adverts from other businesses on your website. You get paid every time somebody clicks on the advert.

⊕   **Private advertising**: You can arrange sponsorship and advertising with businesses, but you will need to prove your website has the volume of visitors to make it worthwhile to prospective advertisers.

Ad Space

If you are planning to put advertising on your website, you will need to include a banner or advertising box. The advertiser will provide you with the code you will need to run their ads.

Above: You can find your own advertisers or use Google AdSense and similar advertising platforms to include banner adverts on your website to make money.

TECHNICAL MATTERS

WEB MANAGEMENT

After lots of hard work, you have created your first website and it is up and running – congratulations! However, the work doesn't stop here. Websites need to be managed, maintained and protected.

TENDING THE GARDEN

Websites need to be looked after. You cannot simply upload your website to a web host and forget about it. Take your eye off the ball and all sorts of things can happen, from your website going down, the page slowing down, to content becoming staid or out-of-date, so it is important to regularly check and maintain your website.

Content

No matter how careful you are, mistakes do happen. Typos and errors can easily slip into your web copy, so it is important to correct these whenever you spot them.

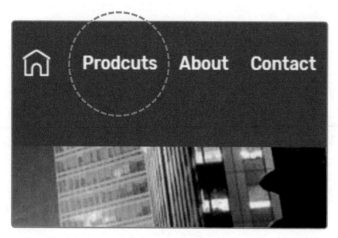

Above: Typos can be embarrassing and look unprofessional.

Content also needs to be kept up to date. If you have a business, any changes, such as a new address, a new product line, or changes to prices, need to be updated. Think about how you can improve your content too. Visitors – and search engines – like fresh, new content, and regularly updating your website's text, images and even layout will help keep your visitors coming back and boost your search-engine rankings.

Calendar

Messenger

Check Email

YAHOO!

What's New

Personalize

Help

claim-your-name.com
claim it before it's gone

☺ **Know when friends are online!**
Click to download Yahoo! Messenger

Yahoo! Mail
free 6MB inbox

[Search] advanced search

Y! Shopping - <u>Father's Day</u> is June 17th **Stores:** <u>Gap</u>, <u>Clinique</u>, <u>Coach</u> and <u>more</u>

<u>Auctions</u> · <u>Classifieds</u> · <u>PayDirect</u> · <u>Shopping</u> · <u>Travel</u> · <u>Yellow Pgs</u> · <u>Maps</u> **Media** **Finance**/<u>Quotes</u> · <u>News</u> · <u>Sports</u> · W
ct <u>Careers</u> · <u>Chat</u> · <u>Clubs</u> · <u>Experts</u> · <u>GeoCities</u> · <u>Greetings</u> · <u>Mail</u> · <u>Members</u> · <u>Messenger</u> · <u>Mobile</u> · <u>Personals</u> · <u>People</u>
sonal <u>Addr Book</u> · <u>Briefcase</u> · **Calendar** · **My Yahoo!** · <u>Photos</u> **Fun** <u>Games</u> · <u>Kids</u> · **Movies** · <u>Music</u> · <u>Radio</u> · <u>TV</u> <u>mor</u>

Yahoo! Auctions - Bid, buy, or sell anything!

Categories
· <u>Antiques</u>   · <u>Computers</u>
· <u>Cameras</u>   · <u>Electronics</u>
· <u>Coins</u>   · <u>Sports Cards</u>
· <u>Comic Books</u> · <u>Stamps</u>

Items
· <u>Allen Iverson</u>   · <u>UBid</u>
· <u>Xena</u>   · <u>Father's Day</u>
· <u>PlayStation 2</u>   · <u>Tomb Raider</u>
· <u>MP3 Players</u>   · <u>Palm Pilots</u>

Baseball Cards - <u>McGwire</u>, <u>A-Rod</u>, <u>Jeter</u>, <u>Bonds</u>, <u>Sosa</u>, <u>Griffey Jr.</u>, <u>Ichiro</u>

Arts & Humanities
<u>Literature</u>, <u>Photography</u>...

Business & Economy
<u>B2B</u>, <u>Finance</u>, <u>Shopping</u>, <u>Jobs</u>...

News & Media
<u>Full Coverage</u>, <u>Newspapers</u>, <u>TV</u>...

Recreation & Sports
<u>Sports</u>, <u>Travel</u>, <u>Autos</u>, <u>Outdoors</u>...

In the News
· <u>Jury awards smoker $3 billion</u>
· <u>U.S. to resume talks with N. Korea</u>
· <u>Judge won't delay McVeigh execution</u>
· <u>Gas supply up, prices falling</u>
· <u>NBA finals</u> - <u>French Open</u>
<u>more...</u>

Marketplace
· new! <u>Consumer Reports</u> - learn before you buy
· Y! Store - build an online

Above: Website fashions change. This older version of Yahoo.com looks seriously outdated now.

Compatibility

Browsers are regularly updated by the companies that produce them, and new devices come onto the market all the time, so make sure you regularly check your website's compatibility with different browsers and devices.

Links

Broken links can frustrate visitors and cause your website to be penalized by search engines. Make sure you check all your internal and outbound links. Any links to pages that no longer exist need to be removed.

Hot Tip

Consider doing a monthly website review. Look at your pages and see if they still look as fresh and attractive as they once did. Websites can go out of fashion, so keep abreast of current trends.

Loading Speed

As you add more content a website can slow down, so it is important to regularly check your page-loading speed (especially as search engines now use this as a basis for search-engine rankings). Tools like Yahoo YSlow, Google Page Speed and Internet Explorer's Page test can help you check your page-loading speed.

Above: You can test your page-loading speed online with websites such as Pingdom.

WEB ANALYTICS

Web analytics is an important part of website management. Tools such as Google Analytics (https://analytics.google.com) and Spring Metrics (www.bigcommerce.co.uk/apps/spring-metrics) can provide you with useful information.

Visitor numbers: Not only should you keep abreast of the number of visitors coming to your website, but knowing where they come from (search-engines searches, adverts, links and so on) can help you plan your advertising and SEO strategies.

Bounce rate: If you are getting a lot of visitors, but people are leaving your website quickly after arriving, it could indicate a problem with your content or design.

Conversions: If lots of people are visiting your e-commerce site but you are not making many sales, this could also indicate a problem with your content, products or pricing.

Start analyzing your site's traffic in 3 steps

1 Sign up for Google Analytics

All we need is some basic info about what site you'd like to monitor.

2 Add tracking code

You'll get a tracking code to paste onto your pages so Google knows when your site is visited.

3 Learn about your audience

In a few hours you'll be able to start seeing data about your site.

Above: It is easy to sign up to Google Analytics and check your website's statistics.

WEB SECURITY

Website security is an important and ongoing consideration for any webmaster. Malware (malicious software) and hackers often target websites, especially e-commerce sites, where they hope to obtain personal or financial data. A malicious attack on your website can lead to several issues:

Jargon Buster

Webmasters are people who look after and maintain websites. If you are designing your own website you will want somebody to maintain it, if you are not doing this yourself.

- **DDoS attack**: A denial of service attack will bombard your website with automated visits preventing real users from accessing it.

- **Website down**: Hackers could make your website unavailable.

- **Data breach**: Hackers can use several techniques to acquire data from your website, such as customers' details.

404

Page Not Found

Above: A 404 Error indicates your website has gone down and is a good indication you have been hacked.

Preventing Security Breaches

Your web host should have some system of security and they are your first port of call if you discover a security breach. Additionally, there is a variety of software available to help keep your website secure, including:

- **Symantec**: www.symantec.com/en/uk/web-security-software. Filters malware threats, blocks URLs with inappropriate content and prevents confidential data loss over web protocols.

- **Sitelock**: www.sitelock.com. Provides a Cloud-based web security system.

- **Site Guarding**: www.siteguarding.com. Protects and removes malware threats from websites and has a free website security checker.

Above: Website security software, such as Symantec, can protect your website from hackers and malicious software (malware).

HTTPS

Secure HTTP (HTTPS) is a protocol used to provide security over the Internet. HTTPS guarantees to users that they are talking to the server they expect, and that nobody else can intercept or change content in transit.

To set up HTTPS you will need a SSL (Secure Sockets Layer) security certificate. These are readily available from places such as www.ssls.com, uk.godaddy.com/offers/ssl-certificate, and www.leaderssl.co.uk for very little cost. You will also need to a dedicated IP address (not a web host sub-domain), on which you can install the SSL certificate, turning your http:// web address into an https:// web address.

Jargon Buster

SSL certificates are small data files that attach a cryptographic key to an organization's details. When installed on a web server, SSL certificates activate the https protocol and allow secure connections from a web server to a browser.

Above: HTTPS or Hyper Text Transfer Protocol Secure.

LEGAL MATTERS

Websites have to adhere to certain rules and regulations, especially business and e-commerce websites, so you need to be sure your website is legal.

WEBSITE LEGALITIES

All websites, and in particular business and e-commerce websites, have to adhere to certain rules, laws and best practices. These vary from country to country, but in general they include such things as:

- **Company information:** For a registered business, the website needs to display the business name, place of registration, registered number and registered office address.

- **Privacy policy:** If a website collects any user data, you have to explain what you will do with that data and prove that the data is protected.

Above: All websites that collect data require a privacy policy. This is Google's.

Web Accessibility and the Disability Discrimination Act: It is a legal requirement that websites should be accessible to people with disabilities, such as those with impaired vision. The World Wide Web Consortium (W3C) has developed a set of standards to ensure websites are built to ensure all can access and operate them.

Cookie Disclaimers

If your website makes use of cookies, it is a legal requirement in the European Union that visitors to your website must be alerted to the fact that cookies are used and what kind of cookies they are. Visitors must also be given the option of opting out of having these cookies placed on their devices. Most websites that use cookies opt for banners or pop-up notifications to present this information.

Above: Websites that use cookies and are accessible to EU residents need a cookie disclaimer. This usually appears at the top, as seen here on the BBC News website.

You can download code and templates to provide this cookie disclaimer from websites such as https://cookieconsent.insites.com and https://cookie-bar.eu.

E-commerce Websites

E-commerce websites have additional laws and requirements they have to abide by:

→ **Terms and conditions**: If you are selling items online you need to specify your delivery and returns policy under the Consumer Protection (Distance Selling) Regulations and Electronic Commerce Regulations (EC Directive).

→ **Credit and debit cards**: If you collect (not through a third party such as PayPal or Worldpay) and process credit and debit card information, you must conform to the Payment Card Industry Data Security Standard.

→ **Email addresses**: EU Anti Spam Laws require you to provide an opt-out instruction on all marketing emails sent to customers.

Other Legal Issues

Websites and blogs can also fall foul of other laws, such as defamation and copyright, so when publishing any content you need to ensure you are not libelling anybody or using content which you do not have permission to use.

Jargon Buster

Cookies are small text files that store information on a visitor's computer. These files store useful information such as log in details or website preferences so a website can remember a visitor.

Online Returns Policy

Online Returns Policy
Returns

This policy is offered in addition to your statutory rights.

Return Address

Good Will Returns Policy

Faulty Goods

Items which can't be returned using our Good Will Returns Policy

How to return your item(s)

International Returns

Above: If you sell products online you will need to outline your returns policy.

TROUBLESHOOTING

Whether your website is live and you run into trouble, or you are still in the design phase but something isn't working, there are several ways to troubleshoot your website.

I CAN'T SEE MY WEBSITE!

This is perhaps the most common issue experienced by webmasters. A website can go down because of a number of issues:

⊖ **DNS**: If you have made any changes to your DNS (domain name server) they can take up to 24 hours to take effect. Also, your domain name may have expired.

Above: A problem with your DNS can cause your website to go down and flag up a DNS error.

→ **DDoS**: A Distributed Denial of Service attack can lead to your website going down. Speak to your web host to see if they have been attacked.

→ **Coding**: Poor code or errors in the code can sometimes lead to a website suddenly going down.

→ **CMS**: If you are using a content management system, then plug-ins, bad code or database issues can cause a website to go down.

> **Hot Tip**
>
> Change the homepage on your web browser to your website, so if it ever goes down you will be quickly alerted.

Validating Your Code

Poor code can lead to all sorts of issues, so it is a good idea to get it checked. Various places online offer this service, including:

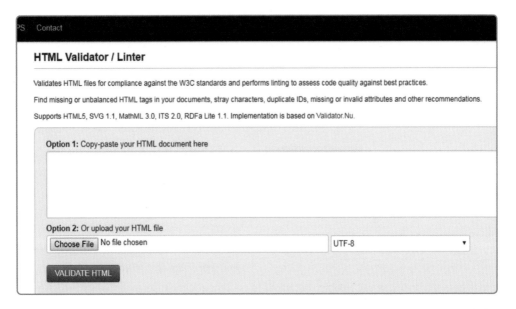

Above: Websites such as Free Formatter not only check for errors but also ensure your HTML abides by W3C standards (World Wide Web Consortium).

- ➔ **Free Formatter**: www.freeformatter. com/html-validator.html. Will check your HTML for errors.

- ➔ **Code Beautify**: https://codebeautify.org/ jsvalidate. Provides JavaScript validation.

- ➔ **CSS Validator**: www.css-validator.org: Checks style sheets for errors.

Jargon Buster

Correcting code is known as 'debugging'. When you are debugging, do not go line by line looking for errors, but concentrate on the areas that are most likely to be the cause.

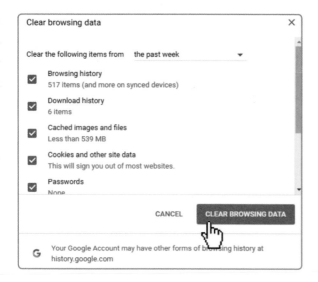

Above: If you cannot see parts of your website, try clearing your browser's cache.

MY CHANGES HAVEN'T TAKEN EFFECT

Browsers make use of a cache system, so many of the images and content on a website can be pre-loaded. If changes to your website do not appear to have been made, try refreshing your browser by pressing Ctrl + F5 or clearing the cache (this is normally in your browser history settings).

MISSING CONTENT

A common problem. Double-check you have uploaded everything to your web host and make sure that all your files, folders and images are on the server. Double-check links to content and their filenames (which are case-sensitive on some web servers). If your homepage is not displaying and you can access other pages, it is possible you have not named your homepage index.html or that it is not in the root folder.

CONNECTIVITY ISSUES

If your website is down, does your email still work? Make sure you rule out simple problems such as your Internet connection going down. Check your browser settings or try to access your website on another browser or device.

DATABASE ERRORS

If you have a database or PHP error, you will often get an explanatory error code when you try to access your website. These error codes can sometimes seem complex, so if you are unsure what an error code means, try putting it in a search engine to find the answer.

Above: It may sound obvious, but make sure you have a web connection before trying to troubleshoot your website.

MOVING A WEBSITE

If you move a website or web page to a new URL, do not worry about people not finding you. You can insert a redirect command between the <HEAD> and </HEAD> tags. See the example below, in which content=1 is a delay of one second, before redirecting.

```
<meta http-equiv="refresh" content=1"; URL=http://
yournewwebaddress.com/">
```

USEFUL WEBSITES

www.barebones.com/products/bbedit
A HTML and text editor for Macs.

www.cmsmadesimple.org
CMS Made Simple will help turn your
designs into web pages.

www.codecademy.com
If you're just starting to learn code, this
website will help you on your journey –
and it's completely free.

www.coffeecup.com/html-editor
CoffeeCup is a HTML and CSS editor
that will help you write code.

www.how-to-build-websites.com/
This web design tutorial can help you
on your way to designing your website.

www.htmlkit.com
A free HTML editor for Windows.

www.javascriptsource.com
You can find ready-made JavaScripts here.

**www.newhorizons.com/courses-and-
certifications/adobe/dreamweaver**
If you're serious about your website

designing skills, you might want to take a
course in Dreamweaver. Different options
can be found here.

www.squarespace.com
A very popular website for starting your
own website.

www.templatemonster.com
Search over 26,000 templates to find
one that will fit your needs.

www.weebly.com
With lots of professional themes to
choose from, Weebly is another great
tool for setting up a website.

www.wix.com
A website to help you create your own
stunning website design for free.

www.wordpress.org
Wordpress will host your blog or website for
you and you can use its WYSIWYG interface
to make changes and updates.

www.w3schools.com/js/
Learn basic to advanced JavaScript with
w3schools.com.

FURTHER READING

Crute, Adam and Johnson, Frederic, *Coding HTML, CSS, JavaScript Made Easy*, Flame Tree Publishing Ltd, 2016

Crute, Adam and Johnson, Frederic, *Coding HTML and CSS*, Flame Tree Publishing Ltd, 2015

Jenkins, Sue, *Web Design All-In-One for Dummies*, John Wiley & Sons, 2013

Krug, Steve, *Don't Make Me Think, Revisited: A Common Sense Approach to Web Usability*, New Riders, 2013

McGrath, Mike, *Coding for Beginners*, In Easy Steps Ltd, 2015

Mischook, Stefan, *Web Design Start Here*, Ilex Press, 2015

Moore, Alannah, *Create Your Own Website The Easy Way*, Ilex Press, 2016

Nahai, Nathalie, *Webs of Influence: The Psychology of Online Persuasion*, Pearson business, 2017

Robbins, Jennifer, *Learning Web Design: A Beginner's Guide to HTML, CSS, JavaScript and Web Graphics*, O'Reilly Media, 2012

Sharma, Amen, *The Google Checklist: Marketing Edition 2016: SEO, Web Design, Paid Advertising, Social Media, PR*, CreateSpace Independent Publishing Platform, 2016

Verou, Lea, *CSS Secrets: Better Solutions to Everyday Web Design Problems*, O'Reilly Media, 2015

Weinschenk, Susan, *100 Things Every Designer Needs to Know About People*, New Riders, 2011

INDEX